Modern Hum

living without ı

by Alfred Hobson
and Neil Jenkins

First published 1989 by Dene Books
Second edition 1993 published by Adelphi Press
Third edition, published in 2000 by North East Humanists
This updated edition published in 2005 by North East Humanists

Further copies available from British Humanist Association
1 Gower Street, London WC1E 6HD
Telephone 0207 –079 3580.
ISBN 0 – 9538120 – 1– 4

Printed by TUPS,
38 Hutton Close, Crowther Industrial Estate,
Washington, NE38 0AH

Foreword to the first edition

In 1976 Bob Griffin, the Secretary of the Tyneside Humanist Society, wrote a short simple guide to modern Humanism. He named it *Humanist Attitudes*, a booklet of over fifty pages in the form of answers to questions – questions which had arisen in the course of many talks on Humanism.

Bob was a remarkable and versatile man. A dedicated schoolteacher, he was a skilled amateur actor and film maker. He conducted the Humanist funeral in a beautiful and moving film *Death of a Miner* which is now in the BBC archives. He was keenly interested in politics and was for some time Chairman of the Newcastle upon Tyne Education Committee. At the age of 65 he stood for Parliament and nearly won the seat for Labour.

He played a leading part in the formation of the Tyneside Humanist Society in the early 1950s and for many years arranged weekly meetings. The many lively discussions influenced the content of *Humanist Attitudes* which had a wide sale in the UK and reached several countries overseas. He died in 1983 at the age of 82, active to the last.

The present authors decided to reissue *Humanist Attitudes* and bring it more up-to-date by including much new thinking. We have consequently renamed it *Modern Humanism*. The original format has been kept of giving a Humanist answer to basic questions. There are of course many more questions than the twenty answered here.

Alfred Hobson
Neil Jenkins

A note on the authors

Alfred Hobson M.Sc. (London) is a retired lecturer in Social Sciences (mainly Economics and Public Administration) from New College, Durham, now retired after many years as Chairman, and later Treasurer, of the Tyneside Humanist Group (now the North East Humanists). He now lives in Kent.

Neil Jenkins Ph.D (Cantab), D.Sc. (Manitoba) is the retired Professor of Oral Physiology from the University of Newcastle upon Tyne, where his main research was on the prevention of tooth decay. He is President of the North East Humanists.

Foreword to the fourth edition

Since its last appearance the text has been updated and expanded, and the reading list has also been enlarged.

I have much appreciated the help given by members of the North East Humanists: Jean and Barrie Berkley, Grace and John Hodge, Gordon Houlsby and Roger McAdam, who have read parts of the manuscript and made helpful suggestions. I am also grateful to Oliver Jenkins for assistance in preparation of the text, and thanks once again to Alan Ball for his cover illustration.

Neil Jenkins
October 2004

Contents

The sections may be read in any order, as they are mostly self-contained and cross-referenced. This book covers a wide range of topics and if readers find a particular section does not hold their interest, then simply move on to another section.

1 WHAT IS HUMANISM?
The origin of the words 'Humanist' and 'Humanism'

A HUMANIST is one who believes that humanity has no need of religion.

It has to be stated that somewhat confusingly, the simple word *Humanist* has been – and still is – applied to many different attitudes and beliefs. To reduce the risk of confusion that can occur from this unfortunate multiplicity of meanings, only the original and present-day meanings are mentioned here. (To explain the complications of the word itself see Nicolas Walter's *Humanism: What's in the Word?*)

Before the Renaissance, the rebirth of the classical knowledge of Greece and Rome that took place during the fourteenth to the seventeenth centuries, European education was chiefly concerned with the study of the Christian religion and preparation for life after death. During the Renaissance opinions changed and liberal education came to consist of the study of Greek and Roman culture. As this was more concerned with the problems facing human beings in their ordinary lives, involving law, geometry, astronomy, medicine and the arts, its followers came to be known as Humanists, a name first used in 1589.

Surprisingly, the word *Humanism* was not used until the early 1800s when it had several different meanings. Today, Humanism refers to those who reject the supernatural views of Christianity and other theistic religions based largely on faith and ancient writings and who concentrate on searching for reasoned answers to the problems facing people during their life. Humanism of this type is variously known as Non-theistic, Scientific, Evolutionary or Secular. In Britain it is now usually known simply as *Humanism* but in America is more often referred to as *Secular Humanism*. The word *secular* has several meanings but as a description of Humanism it means dealing with everyday problems and rejecting supernatural beliefs. It was used first in this sense in 1851 by G. J. Holyoake, the English rationalist and one of the founders of the Co-operative movement.

The main Humanist ideas

Humanists may have very different views on many subjects – they may belong to different political parties, or have widely different backgrounds – but they are all in broad agreement on the following:

a) They see no convincing reasons for belief in a God who created the universe, who controls our lives and who answers prayers (a reason for the appropriateness of the name Humanism).

b) They think that moral ideas arose in the course of evolution rather than being of divine origin. The Humanist criterion for the rightness of an action is the effect of that action on human wellbeing. Actions that raise human wellbeing are right whereas those that reduce human wellbeing are wrong. Humanists are concerned with improving the happiness and welfare of humanity and think that improvement can be brought about by human effort alone not by prayer and supplication – a second reason for use of the name Humanism.

c) They do not take their ideas about the origin and nature of the universe from sacred literature written many centuries ago. Humanists take their view from modern science whose theories are based on observation and experiment. They think that scientific method is the only way of adding to the stock of factual knowledge and discovering the relationship between events, but realise its limited contribution to value judgements (*see page 19*).

d) They see no convincing evidence for the existence of a life after death (or reincarnation, *see page 102*).

e) They continually examine and re-examine knowledge and ideas to consider ways and means of improving the world's environment and the living conditions of humanity and animals.

f) They try to keep their thinking up-to-date by heeding the following warning: Remember that you are human and sometimes make mistakes. Check your facts again and again. Be ready to go over old ground and to test again accepted ideas no matter what weight and authority there is behind them. Do not close your mind in the belief that you have reached the final truth or absolute certainty. New information is being added to the world's knowledge every day and some of it may compel you to change your ideas. Humanists are prepared to admit that they may be wrong.

While there is no Humanist Creed, Humanist organisations do draw up statements from time to time outlining their aims and attitudes to current problems. These are not fixed for all time and may change in the light of new knowledge or ideas. Statements can be obtained from the British Humanist Association (*address in appendix*).

Further reading

Two books in particular should be mentioned which deal comprehensively with almost all the topics discussed in the present text. It seemed unnecessary to list these at the end of each section with other books that had more particular relevance. The two books are Jeaneane Fowler's *Humanism: Beliefs and Practices* (Sussex Academic Press, 1999) and Denis Alexander's *Rebuilding the Matrix: Science and Faith in the Twentyfirst Century* (A Lion Book, 2001).

Other books about Humanism
Herrick, Jim *Humanism: an introduction*
(Rationalist Press Association, 2003)
Kennedy, Ludovic *All In The Mind: A Farewell to God*
(Hodder and Stoughton, 1999)
Lofmark, Carl *Does God Exist?*
(Rationalist Press Association, 1999)
LofmarkCarl *What is the Bible?*
(Rationalist Press Association, 1999)
Norman, Richard *On Humanism* (Routledge, 2004)
Russell, Bertrand *Why I am not a Christian* and *The Faith of A Rationalist*
(A joint publication of these two essays by the National Secular Society

and Rationalist Press Association, first published 1927, republished 1983)
Smoker, Barbara *Humanism*
(British Humanist Association, 1998)
Walter, Nicolas *Humanism: What's in the Word?*
(Rationalist Press Association, 1997)

2 HUMANISM AND OTHER BELIEFS
Is Humanism a Religion?

THE ANSWER TO THIS QUESTION depends on how the word *religion* is defined. To most people in the western world, the idea of religion follows the dictionary definition of 'belief in a higher unseen controlling power and the morality connected therewith'. On this definition, Humanism is clearly not a religion as it rejects belief in the 'higher unseen controlling power'. Many Humanists are very clear that Humanism is not a religion and are unhappy about any attempts to stick the label 'religious' on them. The United Nations in their Charter of Human Rights suggest, on the other hand, that both theistic and non-theistic beliefs can be regarded as religions.

The main features of most of these types of belief are as follows:

1 **Theistic beliefs** are based on the existence of supernatural forces. Their followers accept the existence of a God (or gods and goddesses) whom they regard as the creator of the universe and who is sometimes considered to have the power over matter such as weather, crops, human behaviour and other natural phenomena. In many religions, the deity is a personal God who listens to and answers prayers. These religions are usually associated with a belief in an after-life with rewards and punishments. Traditional Christianity, Judaism and Islam are beliefs of this type.

2 **Non-theistic beliefs** are not based on the supernatural and usually consist of guide-lines for human behaviour which have been drawn up by one or more outstanding thinkers or teachers. Examples are:

a) **Confucianism.** Confucius (551 – 479 BCE*) lived through a chaotic time in China's history. He did not believe in a God or the

---

* BCE stands for *Before Common Era*, a non-religious way of denoting the years traditionally described as *Before Christ*. The letters CE can be substituted for AD where there might be confusion.

soul. He became a teacher and drew up rules for good behaviour based on research into the customs of former times which he thought would provide the basis for a more stable society. His study of the way people behaved led him to formulate one version of the Golden Rule: Do not do to others what you would not like them to do to you.

b) **Buddhism.** Buddha (563 – 483 BCE) drew up rules for behaviour based on practical knowledge and a strong belief in education. He too did not believe in a God or the soul but some of his followers introduced elements of the supernatural into Buddhism. One sect of modern Buddhism with over 11 million followers (mostly in Japan) describes itself as a Buddhist group with Humanist beliefs.

c) **Epicureanism.** Epicurus (342 – 270 BCE) was born on the island of Samos in Ionia – an area noted for philosophers. When he was 18 a short stay in Athens aroused his interest in philosophy and, influenced by Democritus, he established a school of his own, settling in Athens in 307. He taught that the prudent pursuit of pleasure was the main aim in life and that prudence was the real guide to happiness. A prudent person should reason about balancing pain and pleasure in the pursuit of happiness which was defined as 'tranquillity or quiet contentment'. His ideas quickly spread throughout Greece, Asia and Egypt and later they became a major philosophy in Rome – Hadrian, regarded by many as the greatest Roman Emperor, was a devoted Epicurean. Many of the Renaissance Humanists as well as the thinkers of the eighteenth century Enlightenment were Epicureans, for example Rousseau and Voltaire. Later, the ideas of Epicurus were misunderstood and the pursuit of happiness over-emphasised, so that today an Epicurean is regarded by most people as a gourmet – one who delights in expensive foods and wines, rather than in 'quiet contentment'.

In England, a small group of influential people extended the Epicurean idea of personal pleasure to the promotion of general happiness. Their ideas came to be known as Utilitarianism – the ethical principle of 'the greatest good for the greatest number'. The

Utilitarians played a major part in nineteenth century legislation and worked for religious freedom, electoral reform, free trade, easier access to education, reform of the poor law and a reduction in harsh penalties for crime. Most of the leading Utilitarians were rationalists (that is, basing their lives on reason and not on divine revelation) and their leader Jeremy Bentham (1748 – 1832) was a declared atheist. Much of the legislation of the twentieth century has been based on the Utilitarian principle, which is also the inspiration of Humanist ethics.

d) **Other non-theistic beliefs include Stoicism, Rationalism, Positivism, Secularism, Free Thought, Agnosticism and Atheism**.

Secular Humanism, like Confucianism and Buddhism, has a non-theistic set of beliefs. It has a philosophy of life and a framework of beliefs which provide a basis for a moral code so that it does serve the purpose of a religion. Does this give it the status of a religion? Some think it does. Sir Julian Huxley (1887 – 1975), grandson of T.H.Huxley, champion and defender of Darwin, thought that Humanism should be regarded as a non-theistic religion and expressed this view in his book *Religion without Revelation*, published in 1927 and reprinted in 1967. Most Humanists think Humanism should not be described as a religion.

This uncertainty as to the precise nature of Humanism had serious consequences in America when, in 1977, the Supreme Court of Alabama decided that Secular Humanism should have the status of a religion in that state. As the US Constitution forbids the teaching of religion in schools, it was ordered that Secular Humanism could not be taught in Alabama schools, and a number of textbooks could no longer be used as they were alleged to contain Humanist views.

The United Nations Declaration of Human Rights

In 1948 the General Assembly of the United Nations published the Universal Declaration of Human Rights in which Article 18 states that: 'Everyone has the right to freedom of thought, conscience and religion, this right includes freedom to change his religion or belief, and freedom either alone or in company with others and in public or private, to manifest his religion or belief, in teaching, practice, worship and observance'.

This declaration is not legally binding on member nations but they are expected to implement the recommendations. By 1976 the UN had agreed to strengthen and reaffirm the Universal Declaration in the form of two covenants – one on Economic, Social and Cultural Rights and one on Civil and Political Rights. Member nations ratifying these covenants would be legally bound to implement them. In the UK they were ratified in 1976.

In 1981 the UN agreed to the Declaration on the Elimination of all forms of Intolerance and Discrimination based on Religion or Belief. This declaration considerably extended and reinforced the content of Article 18 in the 1948 Universal Declaration of Human Rights.

In 1986 the UN expressed its serious concern that the 1981 Declaration was not being implemented and that there was far too much intolerance and discrimination about religion and belief. The UN therefore appointed a Special Rapporteur to examine the position and a full report was made to the UN in 1987. The report listed the many ways in which intolerance and discrimination were practised and recommended that member states should take legal and administrative measures to eliminate them.

3 THE LIMITS OF HUMAN UNDERSTANDING
If Humanists reject religious ideas, how then can Humanism provide a foundation for a satisfying philosophy of life?

HUMANISM CANNOT PROVIDE ABSOLUTES and certainties for people who crave them. Humanists try to avoid making untestable or unprovable dogmatic or doctrinaire statements. With our present state of knowledge, the universe is known to be so enormously complex that it cannot be fully understood. Those who demand certainties may condemn themselves to disappointment and unhappiness because nobody can provide them with the beliefs they hope for.

Everybody will admit that even the most intelligent animals such as dogs and apes have no conception of many human ideas like politics, ethics or science. The human intellect has developed enormously during the two millions of years in which humanity has been evolving as a separate species. But we have no reason whatever to expect that this has developed sufficiently to enable us to understand fully the nature of the universe or why anything exists. In spite of our great knowledge about the universe, including ideas about how it may have formed, the fact that it exists at all remains an inexplicable mystery. Humanists get used to the idea that the existence of the universe cannot be explained and prefer this to the acceptance of some untestable, mystical explanation such as creation by God. The realisation that there are no absolute certainties need not prevent us from enjoying thoroughly the many sources of happiness that the world can offer. Humanists in general are not puritanical or ascetic. They believe in enjoying to the full natural beauty, human companionship, food, drink, recreations and cultural pursuits – always providing that their activities do not detract from the wellbeing of others.

4 SCIENTIFIC METHOD
What is meant by 'scientific method' and why do Humanists attach so much importance to it?

SCIENTIFIC METHOD IS THE PROCEDURE followed by scientists to investigate the facts of their subject and how they are related to each other. Based on early writings, the procedure has usually been described as follows (but recently this description has been criticised, *see page 15*).

Observations (usually referred to as *data*) about a particular phenomenon are collected and checked for accuracy. Care is taken to ensure that the observations are sufficient in number and chosen randomly.

The observations are then studied to see if any regularities, patterns or generalisations can be found. This process is known as *induction* – drawing general conclusions from individual observations.

Possible explanations – *hypotheses* – are than devised that might account for the general conclusions, it being realised that some of these hypotheses will probably be wrong.

Crucial experiments are then conducted to attempt to decide which hypotheses are wrong and which might be right. In this procedure, two or more similar groups are chosen (which may be of inanimate objects, animals or people). One – *the experimental group* – is subjected to whatever is being tested and the other group – *the control group* – is not. Comparison of the two groups can then decide whether the treatment has had any effect. If so, then the hypothesis is supported but further confirmatory experiments are required to reduce the possibility that errors have occurred.

The procedure is well illustrated by considering experiments carried out by Louis Pasteur in the mid-nineteenth century to investigate the origin of the living things (such as maggots, flies and worms) that grow in stagnant water and decomposing organic matter.

Following the teaching of Aristotle, it had been believed for centuries that these creatures developed by 'spontaneous generation' that is, without living parents – *a first hypothesis*. Some scientists suspected, that these creatures could arise only from pre-existing living things – *a second hypothesis*. These two hypotheses were tested by the very simple experiment of taking two pieces of meat and covering one with several layers of cloth, while the other (the control) was uncovered: both were allowed to stand in a warm environment for several days. The result was that maggots were found on the uncovered (control) meat from flies whose eggs had been laid there, but nothing was found on the covered meat from which, on the first hypotheses, they were supposed to be produced. From this it could be deduced that spontaneous generation did not occur and this was the first indication that a belief which had been held for many generations was obviously mistaken. However – at least on one occasion! – life must have had a spontaneous origin somewhere in the universe and presumably somewhere on Earth (*but see page 35*) when the very first living thing was formed.

When experiments have suggested that a hypothesis is probably correct the next stage is to devise and carry out confirmatory experiments. On the assumption that the hypothesis is correct, predictions are made of the results of these experiments and if the predictions are fulfilled, then the hypothesis is supported though no amount of confirmatory evidence makes a hypothesis completely certain. The process of applying a theory or generalisation to individual cases is known as *deduction*.

When a hypothesis is well established and covers a wide and important subject it is often referred to as a *theory*, such as the atomic theory or the theory of evolution. Confusingly, the terms *hypothesis* and *theory* are often used interchangeably.

An example of confirming a hypothesis by testing a prediction of what should happen if it is true is provided by further experiments by Louis Pasteur. He finally disproved the idea of spontaneous generation by first showing that air contained many bacteria. When air was drawn through a tube containing a plug of cotton wool, living bacteria were retained on the plug. When a fluid, containing substances that would readily putrefy, was boiled to kill any bacteria it contained and then kept in a set of sealed tubes, no putrefaction occurred in any of them even after many months. When bacteria were introduced, either by letting in air or by putting in some of the cotton wool used as a plug, putrefaction occurred within a few days thus showing that living bacteria were necessary for putrefaction.

Pasteur predicted that air on the top of an Alpine mountain, with its limited contact with living things, would contain fewer bacteria than air at ground level. He repeated the experiment with sealed tubes on the top of a high mountain and found that when the mountain air entered a set of twenty tubes containing putrefiable fluid, putrefaction occurred in only one of them. Evidently, the air that entered nineteen of the tubes contained no bacteria or too few to cause putrefaction within the duration of the experiment, thus confirming the hypothesis.

Deduction from well-established hypotheses is the basis of the solution of practical problems in applied science and technology. From the example just given, deduction from the hypothesis that putrefaction arises from bacteria in the air led to methods of food preservation and the prevention of infection in wounds.

The reluctance of scientists to accept new ideas

Pasteur's denial that spontaneous generation ever occurred was hotly contested by some of his fellow scientists. This is one of the many examples in the history of science showing that, contrary to the spirit of scientific method, scientists are sometimes reluctant to accept new ideas that contradict their previous pattern of thought. Even Einstein, one of the greatest scientific geniuses of all time, never fully accepted quantum theory.

Proof versus falsification

Sir Karl Popper (1902-1994), one of the most distinguished of recent philosophers, emphasised that it is never possible to prove the validity of a hypothesis with absolute certainly. It may, however, be possible to disprove, or, to use Popper's term, to falsify it. As experiments or new facts falsify incorrect hypotheses, they are rejected and those that remain may possibly be correct – though in the light of further knowledge they too may be rejected or modified in their turn.

The nature of scientific laws

In the early days of science, the conclusions induced from observations (the second stage above) were thought to be based on divine commands as to how the universe worked. They were called *laws,* such as Newton's *Law of Gravity* and Kepler's *Laws of Planetary Motion*. Like all scientific ideas, they are subject to change or rejection in the light of new evidence.

The nature of scientific laws is a deep philosophical mystery. Are they built into nature, as some scientists believe, and if so, how did they arise? Others think, however, that (as Paul Davies puts it) 'the laws are basically the result of human observations and are imposed on the world by our minds in order to make sense of it'. These unanswered questions are discussed in more detail by Paul Davies in *The Mind of God* and John Barrow in *Theories of Everything.*

The problem of induction

The fact that scientific method is based on induction presents a problem, namely, that the validity of induction depends on certain assumptions such as the 'uniformity of nature'. How do we know that this assumption is correct and that observations and conclusions made in one place at one time are valid in other places and other times? Only by making more observations and drawing conclusions by induction! Thus scientific method, based on induction, depends on the validity of assumptions that are themselves supported only by more induction – something which critics of scientific method have pointed out. The scientific answer is, of course, that the results obtained by scientific method have been applied to technology with outstanding success thus showing that, in practice, scientific method works.

Popper's criticism of 'classical' scientific method

Popper has suggested that, in practice, scientists do not usually follow the procedure outlined above. He thought that it is not the collection of data that usually leads to the formulation of hypotheses but rather curiosity aroused by thinking about some well-established phenomenon or about data already collected by others. On Popper's view, the forming of the hypothesis is the *first* stage of scientific method followed by carrying out experiments or collecting data to falsify or support the hypothesis. The two procedures can be contrasted as follows. In 'classical' scientific method, a mass of data is collected and an attempt made to sort it out into a generalisation or law whose validity is then tested by experiment. Popper's approach would be: I wonder if X can be explained by Y or Z – let's carry out some experiments to find out! Popper believes that his procedure is not based on induction and hence avoids the logical flaw mentioned above. However, Popper does not seem to be historically correct in his view because some scientific theories did arise from data that had already been collected before the theory was formulated and were, therefore, based on induction. One example is the theory of evolution, published in 1859 in *The Origin of Species*. Darwin states in his autobiography: 'My first notebook was opened in 1837. I worked on truly Baconian principles and without any theory collected facts on a wholesale scale ... by printed enquiries, by conversation with skilful breeders and gardeners, and by extensive reading'.

Popper's idea of scientific method was criticised by Thomas Kuhn (1922-1996) on the grounds that the history of science showed that his procedure was not often used. Far from trying to falsify theories, Kuhn claimed that many scientists 'explain away' criticisms or find additions to their own theory to make it more feasible and are reluctant to admit that they are wrong. Kuhn argues that the progress of science depends on the formation of a *paradigm* – defined as a body of ideas shared by a group of scientists, and what Kuhn describes as 'normal science' consists of trying to solve any puzzles in the paradigm. If results arise which do not fit the paradigm, it is abandoned and a new paradigm proposed. An example of this procedure has been shown above: the widely held belief (paradigm) in spontaneous generation was abandoned in favour of Pasteur's demonstration of the continuity of life from other living things. This is what Kuhn calls a 'scientific revolution'; the new paradigm is also subject to review and may also be replaced.

Origins of scientific method

The procedures of induction and deduction were first introduced by Aristotle (384–322 BCE). However, Confucius (551– 479 BCE, *see page 5*) is reputed to have taught that 'Learning undigested by thought is labour lost; thought unassisted by learning is perilous'. This is a good summary of the ideas underlying scientific method made some 150 years before Aristotle – though he would not be aware of it because little was known about China in the West until the thirteenth century. Aristotle's ideas were modified by a number of mediaeval thinkers among whom the thirteenth century Franciscan monk Roger Bacon (c.1214–1292) introduced the idea of experiment, as opposed to speculation and argument, as the main source of knowledge. His namesake, Francis Bacon (1561–1626) is often regarded as the 'father' of scientific method. Although he did no scientific work himself he had great literary skills and his book *Novum Organum* of 1620 made a great impact. In it he emphasised the importance of not jumping to conclusions too quickly and of avoiding prejudice (Aristotle had been prone to both these errors).

He also pointed out the importance of experiments and the value of science in producing new inventions and gaining a mastery over nature.

Contrasting skills of the scientist

It is not always realised that scientific research involves two contrasting skills. In collecting data or recording the results of experiments great accuracy and the absence of bias or prejudice are necessary. Scientists must record what they see, not what they would like to see, and much of this work can be a dull routine. In formulating hypotheses, on the other hand, a lively imaginative mind is required that is prepared to consider ideas from any source. In addition to disciplined thinking, useful ideas can come from hearsay, hunch and even dreams (at least one scientist has reported that the basis of an important idea came to him in a dream). But, having received ideas from whatever source, they must be subjected to strict experimental tests. The outstanding scientific geniuses are those with lively, inventive minds who can picture familiar things in a completely new light. Because few scientists excel in both making meticulous observation and in forming imaginative hypotheses and because different types of expertise are often involved in modern research, most of it is now done by groups of scientists working as a team.

Bias and how it is avoided

Although ideally scientists should rid their minds of any bias or prejudice while carrying out experiments, in practice there is nearly always some reason for hoping for a particular result, even if this is only subconscious. Scientists who are testing their own hypotheses naturally hope that they are correct and that their experiment will support them and they may have an even stronger hope for a negative result if they are testing the hypothesis of a rival scientist! Also a great deal of research is carried out in industry where the hope is that a particular product will be effective or is superior to that of another firm. Although modern research methods, using automatic recording instruments and statistical analysis, can certainly reduce the risk that bias will affect the results – the interpretation of these results can still be influenced by the wishes and hopes of the researcher. Scientists are fully aware of this tendency and take precautions to avoid bias by carrying out, as far as is possible, what are called *blind experiments*. In this procedure, the scientist who is comparing the experimental and control results does not know which is which. Suppose, for example, the effect of a fertiliser on plant growth is being tested. The scientist who measures the growth of the plants receiving the fertiliser (the experimental group) and those that were not (the control group) would not be told which group each plant belonged to until the measurements had been completed.

Although bias can be largely avoided or allowed for, there are on record a few scandals of dishonest scientists who deliberately misreported their results.

Why Humanists attach so much importance to scientific method

Humanists regard scientific method as important because it is now recognised as the most reliable means of investigating factual questions (*but see page 13*) and replaces the traditional sources of authority like Aristotle (regarded for centuries as an infallible source of knowledge) or divine revelation as recorded in sacred writings. Owing to the uncertainties of scientific observations and of the conclusions drawn from them, scientific knowledge is never final or complete and should be regarded as nothing more than the most probable conclusion from the available data.

It must be emphasised that the realm of scientific method is confined to facts and if, for any reason, scientific method cannot be applied to a factual question (such as the nature of consciousness) then that question must be left open. Scientists should always be prepared to admit that they don't know the answer to a question if the evidence does not suggest one.

Facts versus values

A great deal of everyday life is concerned not with *facts*, but with *values* – such as happiness, beauty or moral rectitude and here the application of science is very limited. Scientific method cannot provide decisions on values; there is no scientific way of deciding whether one object is more beautiful than another or whether one type of behaviour is more morally correct than another. This distinction is a complicated philosophical problem, and has been summarised by the BHA Philosophers' Group as 'Facts about the world are there to be discovered, values are things we choose, create or invent.' An indication of values chosen, created or invented by Humanists are discussed on pages 54-9.

Science can, however, investigate factual questions about value judgements. For example, opinion polls can find out whether education has any effect on ideas about, say, abortion, or whether income level makes any difference to such things as taste in music.

Further reading
Barrow, John D. *Theories of Everything*
(Vintage, 1992)
Chalmers, AF *What is This Thing Called Science?*
(Open University Press, 1978)
Clegg, Brian *The First Scientist; The visionary genius of Roger Bacon*
(Constable and Robinson, 2002)
Davies, Paul *The Mind of God*
(Penguin 1992)
Humanist Philosophers' Group *What Is Humanism ?*
(BHA, 2002)
Kuhn, Thomas *The State of Scientific Revolution*
(University of Chicago Press, 1962)
Losee, John *A Historical Introduction to the Philosophy of Science*
(Oxford University Press, 1993)
Magee, Bryan *Popper*
(Fontana, 1973)
Warburton, Nigel *Philosophy: The Basics (*Chapter 5*)*
(Routledge, 1995)

5 THE BEGINNING AND END OF THE WORLD
How do scientists account for the beginning of the
world and how do they think it will end?

DURING THE HISTORY of the human race, many thinkers have formed ideas about how the world began, how it will end and what will happen to the people then living. Originally these ideas were probably in the form of stories. Perhaps they were made up and told out of a natural delight in story-telling. Many people like to have an explanation of some sort for everything, even if, in the pre-scientific age, it was little more than a folk tale or a fairy story. It is possible that what were originally told purely as stories for enjoyment became through years of retelling fossilised into religious beliefs.

Today, we can see that story-telling about how the world began was bound to fail. The traditional attitude was that, in the beginning, an all-powerful God created the universe and the world 'out of nothing'. Humanists argue that the hypothesis of a creator God may have been useful in the past but today leads to more problems than it solves. In particular, if an all-powerful God created the universe, why did He do so and what brought about the existence of the all-powerful God in the first place?

Unfortunately, the words 'universe' 'world' and 'galaxies' are used in different senses. *Universe* sometimes means the whole of everything that exists, now better known as 'the cosmos'. *Universes* (plural) refers to the island universes, the groups of millions of stars originally described as spiral nebulae. The *world* can be a synonym for Earth, but can also refer to other planets (as in 'other worlds'). A galaxy is a group of stars, but the *Galaxy* (with a capital G) refers to our own Galaxy, our own group of stars, visible on a dark night's cloudless sky as a faint band of light (the 'Milky Way').

Humanists accept the scientific view of the origin and end of the world, of which the following is a very brief account. Over the last hundred years, astronomers using very much improved telescopes (optical, radio and the satellite-based Hubble Space Telescope) have been able to find out a great deal about the size and nature of the universe and work out hypotheses about its origin and development. The question of the mechanism of the creation of the universe was, until the 1970s, regarded as beyond the scope of science and even beyond all human understanding. If creation is thought about as a common-sense problem there would seem to be only two ways in which it might be solved and both of these seem impossible! It might be thought, firstly, that the matter of the universe has always existed and had no beginning or time of creation. However, the minds of non-mathematicians cannot picture this possibility. On the other hand it is equally difficult to imagine the alternative – that matter was created out of nothing at one moment in time. But it must be assumed that one of these ideas contains the truth, in spite of the difficulties.

Most scientists who study the origin of the universe now think that the second view is the more probable and that matter, time and space were created about 13.7 billion years ago (that is, 13,700,000,000 years) in what is called (at first jokingly) the Big Bang. When the Big Bang was suggested nobody could speculate how matter/energy (*see page 29*) could be created out of nothing. In 1973 the idea was mooted that creation might have occurred by a process known as a 'quantum fluctuation', but it was not followed up or taken seriously until the 1980s. This is too complicated and abstruse to be described here but is explained by Paul Davies in his book *God and the New Physics*. The proponents of this hypothesis think that quantum fluctuations could create matter/energy out of nothing: this may sound like a miracle but is not regarded as impossible on the basis of quantum theory and does not require the intervention of anything resembling a creator God. Other scientists think that this overstates the case and that the universe must have contained 'something to fluctuate' (the origin of which cannot be explained) before the Big Bang occurred. Obviously these speculations on the very boundaries of knowledge and thought must be regarded as tentative, but future work maybe expected to clarify them. Why the Big Bang occurred and why anything exists at all remain inexplicable.

It is thought that, in the tiniest fraction of a second after its creation, the newly-formed matter expanded from atomic size to about the size of a grapefruit (a process called *inflation*) after which the expansion slowed down greatly, but is still continuing right up to the present time and is accelerating. The present expansion is not the outward movement of matter through space, but the expansion of space itself carrying matter with it. The main evidence for the continuing expansion is based on the analysis by the spectroscope of the light from the distant galaxies. This shows what is called a *red shift* which is interpreted as meaning that the galaxies are moving away from each other and from Earth (but Earth is not, of course, the central point from which the galaxies are moving). This means that the universe is expanding at a rate that can be calculated from the size of the red shift and, by working backwards, it is possible to estimate approximately when the Big Bang occurred and the expansion began. The answer that emerges is 13.7 billion years ago. The Big Bang should still only be regarded as a hypothesis although there are several lines of evidence for it and it is widely accepted. The state of the Big Bang theory can best be judged by noting a most unusual statement issued in May 2004 by 33 astronomers from ten countries. They complained that so much support is given to studies relevant to the Big Bang that alternative theories are being neglected. They asserted that, contrary to the spirit of free enquiry, scientists who were critical of the Big Bang are afraid to speak out for fear of losing financial support.

The result of the Big Bang

After its rapid inflation phase, the Big Bang is thought to have resulted in the formation of a vast swirling mass of the gases hydrogen and helium. For reasons not yet understood, this swirling mass divided up into separate clouds of matter that formed the spiral nebulae. Originally these faint patches of light between some of the stars were thought to be masses of gases, but using one of the most powerful telescopes in the world, Edwin Hubble in the 1920s confirmed previous suggestions that these spiral nebulae were made up of myriads of stars. These groups of stars are sometimes called 'island universes' because they are separated in space from each other and from our own Galaxy. It is probable that some of these stars are surrounded by planets (*see page 35*). Our Galaxy, popularly known as the Milky Way, has a disc shape and contains about 100,000 million stars and is estimated to rotate about its axis every 225 million years. Hundreds of millions of other similar galaxies are known to exist throughout the universe. The sun is a typical medium-sized star situated about one third of the way between the outer edge of our Galaxy and its centre. The stars appear fainter than the sun simply because they are millions of times further away from Earth than is the sun.

The fate of Earth and of living things on it

Stars do not last forever – they form, emit energy while evolving through various stages and eventually, it is believed, most will end up as cold 'dead' worlds. In about seven billion years our sun will begin to burn out. As it does so, astronomers think, it will expand into a type of star known as a red giant followed by a contraction into another type of star known as a white dwarf which, over millions of years, will cool down to a dark, inert body. During the red giant stage Earth will become too hot to support life and all living things will become extinct. As some stars go through the terminal stages of this cycle, others are being formed from gas and dust in the space between the stars.

Fortunately, the time scale of these changes is so unimaginably vast that the final prospect of a dead Earth need not be a matter of concern to us or interfere with our present happiness or enjoyment of life. The fossil record shows that, several times during the history of life on Earth, massive extinctions of many species have occurred. In one of these, some 65 million years ago, the dinosaurs became extinct, along with about two-thirds of the other species then living (*see page 42*). From geological evidence, that incident appears to have been caused by the impact of an asteroid which fell on what is now Mexico.

The asteroids (also known as minor planets) are a group of over five thousand bodies ranging in size from the largest, 560 miles across, to others as small as a few hundred feet across. They move round the sun, mostly between the orbits of Mars and Jupiter, but some have irregular orbits and cross the orbit of Earth. One small asteroid came within 70,000 miles of Earth (a very small distance in astronomical terms) in December 1994.

A large area in north-west India is covered by many layers of lava also found to be about 65 million years old. This indicates that a 'supervolcano' erupted, in which thousands of cubic kilometers of lava and debris would be ejected over a large area. Geologists think that such an event occurred three times (at intervals of 600,000 years) during the last two million years. The last supervolcano originated in what is now the Yellowstone Park area of North America and the recently recorded instability in that region suggests that a similar eruption is due any time during the next few thousand years. The impact and the supervolcano would have caused widespread fires and the resulting smoke as well as dust from the shattered asteroid and from the Earth's surface would block out the sun, probably for many months or even years, stopping plant growth and starving any surviving large animals such as the dinosaurs.

The probability of future impacts and possible preventive measures

A missile comparable with the object that caused the extinction of the dinosaurs has been calculated to have been about six miles in diameter. From observations of the number, size and orbits of asteroids the probable frequency of such impacts is estimated to be about one every hundred million years. Smaller objects, still large enough to cause global damage to life after collision, may be expected about three times every million years. Impacts with even smaller objects are believed to occur much more frequently – once or twice a century in one estimate. Their effect would be devastating over only a few hundred square miles, as occurred in Tunguska, Siberia, in 1908 and in an area further east in Siberia in 1947. Fortunately, none has been known to fall on populated areas but if one did it would be locally catastrophic. These considerations suggest that life on Earth may become extinct long before the sun becomes a red giant.

The possibility within the next few thousand years of an impact leading to serious disruption of civilisation and massive loss of life cannot be dismissed but it is to be hoped that two activities will be expanded on an energetic scale. First, more resources should be made available to astronomers who are studying the orbits of potential missiles so that humankind might have some years' notice of a collision. Secondly, physicists, including some that were engaged in 'star wars' research (methods of destroying nuclear missiles before they reach their target) are now considering possible ways of destroying or diverting asteroids or other objects in space whose orbits indicate that they are on a collision course with Earth.

Further reading

Davies, Paul *God and the New Physics*
(Penguin, 1993)
Greco, Peter *Collision Earth!* (Blandford, 1998)
Gribbin, Mary and John *Being Human* (Phoenix, 1993)
Hawking, Stephen *A Brief History of Time* (Bantam Press, 1988)
and *The Universe in a Nutshell* (Bantam Press, 2001)
Moore, Patrick *An Atlas of the Universe* (Phillips, 1997)
Steel, Duncan *Rogue Asteroids and Doomsday Comets*
(John Wiley and Sons, 1995)

6 'THE GROUND OF OUR BEING'
If Humanism is not based on belief in God what is it based on?

WITH THE DEVELOPMENT OF SCIENCE, especially during the last hundred years, the idea of a God as a superhuman being living somewhere in outer space has become increasingly difficult to sustain. Consequently, for many years, Christians have been searching for a more realistic and up-to-date definition of God. The Church of England in 1987 accepted that its members could hold a variety of views on Christian beliefs.

Paul Tillich (1886 – 1965) was a German theologian who left Germany in 1933 to settle in the USA. Tillich rejected the idea of a personal, all-knowing and all-powerful God with a superhuman brain as something that was too abstract. Instead, he defined God as the *'ground of our being'* which has led to much debate among Christians. This question might therefore be reworded: What do Humanists think is the 'ground of our being'? In answer they would turn to the scientist.

Before discussing this, a short digression on the structure of matter may be helpful.

The structure of matter

The building blocks from which all the matter in the universe is made consist of some 90 naturally occurring substances (and some additional man-made ones) called *elements*. An element is a substance that cannot be split into simpler substances by ordinary chemical methods. The elements are made up of particles called *atoms*, with a typical diameter of one hundred millionth of a centimetre, defined as the smallest particle of an element with the properties of that element. The weights of the atoms of each element (the *atomic weight*) are all different and are compared by taking the weight of the atom of oxygen to be 16. Atomic weights of the elements range from 1.008 for the simplest element, hydrogen, to 238 for the most complicated of natural elements, uranium. If the atom of a radioactive element is split up (as occurs in nuclear reactors and in natural radioactivity) the resulting pieces become atoms of different elements. For example, atoms of the radioactive element radium (atomic weight 226) break up spontaneously through many stages into helium (atomic weight 4) and lead (atomic weight 206).

When two or more identical atoms unite, they form a *molecule.* For example, two atoms of oxygen bound together form a molecule of oxygen. If the atoms are of different elements they become molecules of a compound – for example, two atoms of hydrogen combined with one of oxygen form a molecule of the compound water (H_2O).

Chemistry and its subdivisions

Chemistry is the study of the elements and their compounds. Its three subdivisions are *inorganic chemistry* – the study of all the elements and their compounds except those of carbon, *organic chemistry* – the study of carbon compounds, and *biochemistry* – the study of the composition of living things and the chemical changes (metabolism) occurring in living things.

In the early days of chemistry, it was thought that substances that came from plants and animals (almost all of which are compounds of carbon) could only be obtained from living things and they were called organic compounds and the study of them therefore became known as organic chemistry. Later, it was discovered that some organic compounds could be made in the laboratory so the term organic chemistry now refers to the study of compounds of carbon whether they are normally produced by living things or not: the term *organic chemistry* is therefore rather misleading.

Matter and energy are inter-convertible

Physicists have shown that, in suitable circumstances, the matter that makes up the universe can be changed into energy and vice versa. Thus, the fundamental basis of the universe (the *'ground of our being'*) may be referred to as matter/energy. The following shows one way in which this conversion may happen and is the cause of the immense energy of the hydrogen bomb as well as being one of the sources of heat in the sun and other stars. When hydrogen atoms (atomic weight 1.008) are forced together at extremely high temperatures, each group of four atoms bind together to become one helium atom which weighs slightly less (4.003) than the four hydrogen atoms (4x1.008 = 4.032). The 0.7% of the weight of the hydrogen atoms not required to form the helium atoms is converted into very large quantities of energy. The energy released from 1 gram of hydrogen when it is converted into helium is three million times greater than that released when 1 gram of coal is burned.

Implications of the importance of matter/energy

Humanists are materialist in the philosophical sense, in that they believe that matter/energy is primary, and that mind, intellect and emotion arise from matter/energy, and have no separate existence. This belief is known as *monism* – soul and body cannot be separated – and contrasts with the religious belief in *dualism* (the view that the soul can exist separately from the body). *See also page 45.* It is important to clarify that when stating that Humanists are philosophical materialists, this should not be confused with the everyday sense of *materialist* – individuals whose chief interests are in pursuing money and material things.

So if asked the question *'What is the ground of our being?'*, Humanists might reply, 'It is the existence of matter/energy moulded by natural forces into living things on one of the planets surrounding the Sun, just one of the hundred thousand million stars in our Galaxy'.

Further reading
Robinson, John *Honest To God*
(SCM 1963)
Robinson, John and Edwards, David *The Honest To God Debate*
(SCM 1963)

Ryle, Gilbert *The Concept of the Mind*
(Hutchinson 1949, with many reprints by Penguin Books). *A philosophic
exposition of monism which had great influence when first published.*

7 THE ORIGIN OF LIFE
What do scientists know about the origin of life?

THE FUNDAMENTAL NATURE of life itself cannot be defined. This may seem a surprise to most people, as it is generally quite apparent whether a thing is alive or dead. But it follows that this causes obvious difficulties in proposing a theory for the first starting of life.

Possible mechanisms for some of the *earlier* steps have been suggested and have gained some experimental support. It might be speculated that at some stage one or more constituents were synthesized or there occurred one or more changes in the environment (such as acidity or osmotic pressure) which made possible the beginnings of life.

The structure of living things

Biochemists have shown that the cells that make up the bodies of living things, including human beings, are made up of atoms and molecules of the same kind as make up the rest of the universe. Most cells contain about 70% of water and consist of a nucleus surrounded by the cytoplasm – a very complex mixture of salts, several thousand different types of proteins and many other substances dissolved in water. Proteins are large molecules made up of hundreds, or even thousands, of molecules of twenty different substances called amino acids linked together like a chain, in some cases folded into complicated shapes, which, along with water, make up most of the weight of cells. Cells are surrounded by a membrane made up of two layers of fatty substances and some protein: it holds the cell together and lets food in and waste products out.

Within the nucleus are the chromosomes (in human cells, 46 in number) consisting of very long molecules of deoxyribonucleic acid (DNA) arranged in a double helix, rather like two spiral staircases twisted around each other. The 46 chromosomes contain the genes, which differ considerably in size and therefore contain different numbers of genes. It is now estimated that human chromosomes contain a total of about 30,000 genes, not 100,000 as previously thought. Genes exert their influence by the formation of proteins; by coding which amino acids enter each protein and the order in which they are linked.

An unsolved problem is how the incredibly complicated genetic code itself has evolved, leading even some scientists to think that it must have been divinely controlled. However, Dawkins, in *The Blind Watchmaker,* has argued that, given the millions of years over which it probably evolved, the formation of the genetic code by chance alone cannot be dismissed.

The nature and amount of each protein formed by the genes determines such details as the colour of the hair and the shape of the nose as well as the immense complexity of an individual's personality (*see page 65*). DNA has the important property of forming copies of itself (replicating) whenever a cell divides during growth; each copy enters and passes on its genetic information to the new cell formed from the division.

Cells vary greatly in size, shape and specialised function in different tissues such as bone cells, blood cells, nerve cells, but the size of most human cells range between 0.01 and 0.03 mm in diameter. There are many species of animals that consist of one cell only. These are known as the protozoa, and the amoeba is often taken as a typical example. Most animals contain a very large number of cells – an adult human body is thought to contain several hundred million million cells.

The problems of life arising from non-living material

The following is a brief description of how a few of the main stages might have occurred but at which step life really began is not known.

Surprisingly, some simple organic substances, such as carbon monoxide, formaldehyde, cyanide and ammonia, are known to be present in the stars and in space. Presumably these simple substances are formed quite readily in the absence of living things. It was shown in experiments in the 1950s that if electric sparks are passed through what was then believed to be the earth's atmosphere when life was beginning (mixtures of water, hydrogen, methane and ammonia) for several days, amino acids, the building blocks of proteins, are formed. This mixture of gases is no longer believed to have been the atmosphere of the early earth, so the importance of this experiment is now uncertain.

It is quite likely that, billions of years ago, the hot steamy shallow seas (which were called, at first rather jokingly, the *primordial soup*) and the atmosphere above it contained these simple substances and it has been speculated that lightning flashes and ultraviolet light from the sun provided sufficient energy to produce amino acids. The substances that make up DNA were also probably formed at the same time and in the same way. The next step – the building up of proteins from the amino acids – is more difficult to envisage. In living cells, most of the chemical activities such as forming proteins, other cell constituents and releasing energy from fats and sugars, are carried out by the action of substances, themselves proteins, called enzymes. Proteins are formed by joining amino acids together by enzymes interacting in a most complicated way with DNA. How could proteins form in the primordial soup in the absence of both enzymes and DNA? There is no certain answer but very short chains of amino acids – much shorter than those in living cells – have been shown to form when solutions resembling primordial soup are evaporated, as might happen on the shores of lakes and seas. It is not unreasonable to speculate that during the hundreds of millions of years that elapsed before life began that larger molecules of proteins were formed in the same way and by a process of natural selection those that were most stable and could most readily be converted into larger chains would survive. Eventually some of the early proteins probably acquired the special structures that enable them to act as enzymes, after which protein formation would be greatly facilitated. It must be admitted that the formation of 'full size' proteins has never been produced in the laboratory from non-living matter.

The next step in the development of life would be the surrounding of the DNA-protein complex with a membrane to form something resembling a primitive cell. This process is not too difficult to imagine once fatty substances had been evolved (these fatty substances tend to form globules quite spontaneously, not unlike the walls surrounding cells). It would be expected that some of the globules would entrap DNA and the other substances concerned with forming proteins. This could lead to the earliest single celled organisms from which, it is believed, were evolved the millions of species of plants and animals that live or have lived on earth. There is wide agreement that the earth was formed about 4.5 billion years ago and structures that look like the fossils of cells have been described in rocks aged about 3.8 billion years, suggesting that life established itself within 700 million years of the earth's formation and this has become widely accepted.

However, it has been questioned whether these structures are fossils of cells because 'black smokers' – rocks formed in volcanic outlets on the bed of the ocean – contain crystals easily mistaken for fossil cells. Earlier it was thought that bacteria could not live in very hot environments as these seemed incompatible with life. Rocks several kilometers below the surface of the Earth, and black smokers, are much more like the land surface of the Earth before it had cooled down. This suggests the possibility that life may have begun, not in the dilute primordial soup, but far below the surface, where it would have been protected from the intensely dangerous radiation from outer space.

The possibility of life elsewhere in the universe

One view about the possibility of extra-terrestrial life is that, since life has formed once in a suitable, if rare, environment it is likely to have developed several or even many times if there are planets surrounding other stars. The red shift (*see page 23*) of a few of our nearest stars have detected periodic fluctuations, or wobbles, that could be explained by the gravitational pull of planets. Modern telescopes have revealed bodies resembling planets (although larger than the planets in our solar system) associated with more than a hundred stars (at the time of writing, mid-2004). The total number of stars is so vast that suitable conditions probably do exist, or have existed in the past, in at least some places in the universe, but we have as yet no direct evidence for this.

Others think that living things are so complicated and the events leading to life are so improbable that they are unlikely to have occurred more than once. A further view is that life probably formed only in one place but travelled, perhaps as spores, through space to wherever it now exists. Although this is an old idea it has seldom been taken seriously. It has received renewed attention in recent years in view of the finding of organic substances in space, in comets and in meteorites and the presence of what some scientists have interpreted as fossilised bacteria in a meteorite believed to have come from Mars. Although the idea of life travelling through space is regarded as highly improbable some scientists think it cannot be ruled out altogether. For a full discussion of *panspermia,* as this idea is called, see Paul Davies's book *The Fifth Miracle.*

Attempts since 1960 to communicate by radio with possible inhabitants of planets orbiting other stars (SETI, the Search for Extra-Terrestrial Intelligence) have not been successful. Of course, even if intelligent beings do exist on other planets, there is no means of knowing whether their development has led to a technological society similar to our own enabling them to receive our radio messages, and even if this is so, whether their development coincides in time with ours.

If intelligent life is ever detected elsewhere in the universe it will have a profound effect on human thought — scientifically, philosophically as well as theologically! The possibility of the existence of extra-terrestrial beings has led to some theologians debating whether, if they do exist, would they be sinful like humankind and, if sinful, would Christ's sacrifice on Earth cover them as well? The director of the Vatican Observatory, whose work includes the search for planets orbiting other stars, thinks that God may have saved them but perhaps from some other method rather than a sacrifice like that of Christ.

Further reading
Davies, Paul   *Are We Alone?*
(Penguin, 1995)
Davies, Paul   *The Fifth Miracle*
(Allen Lane, The Penguin Press, 1998)
de Duve, Christian   *Vital Dust*
(Basic Books, New York, 1995)
Dyson, Freeman   *Origins of Life*
(Cambridge University Press, 1995).
Smith, John Maynard and Szathmanry, Eors   *The Origins of Life: From the birth of life to the origins of language*
(Oxford University Press, 1999)

8 THE EVOLUTION OF LIVING THINGS
How do scientists think that plants, animals and people came into being?

CHARLES DARWIN, one of Humanism's heroes, made two important statements that transformed human thought in the mid-1800s. Following his five-year voyage round the world in HMS Beagle and his visits to many countries Darwin accumulated an enormous amount of information about natural things, which, when sorted out, provided overwhelming evidence that evolution had occurred from the simplest living things to produce the millions of species of higher plants and animals now on the Earth, including humanity. This was the first time that people were introduced to the fact that humanity was no more than one of the species of these animals.

Darwin also suggested a mechanism by which evolution occurred and there is general agreement among scientists that Darwin's theory of natural selection, or the 'survival of the fittest', is the main process by which plants and animals have evolved. It must be pointed out that fitness in the evolutionary sense has the specialised meaning of fitness to have offspring'. Evolution is not necessarily affected by fitness in the ordinary sense: people good at physical jerks or animals that run faster than usual do not influence evolution unless their achievements enable them to live longer and rear offspring more successfully.

Darwin during his lifetime did accept the possibility of additional mechanisms and later editions of his famous book, *The Origin of Species*, suggested that Lamarck's idea of inheritance of acquired characteristics might be a factor in evolution. This idea has been disbelieved for many years because changes occurring during life do not affect the genes of the sex cells and would not therefore be expected to affect the offspring, upon which evolution depends.

Natural selection in evolution

Most species are very prolific in reproducing themselves, giving rise to far more offspring than can possibly survive. Survival can be influenced in two main ways. The first that is believed to have played a part in evolution is change in the environment, such as climate or availability of food. Following such a change some species, or members of a species, will possess inherited characteristics that make them able to adjust to the change better than others and thus they will survive and reproduce at the expense of the less able. For example, it was found that when industrialisation advanced over the nineteenth century, light-coloured trees and walls became darker from deposits of soot or because lichens were killed by the pollution. In such areas inhabited by light and dark coloured moths, the proportion of dark moths gradually increased, because, compared with the light moths, they were less able to be seen and eaten by predators and thus would survive and produce more offspring. In this case, a natural genetic variation influenced survival following a change in the environment.

The role of mutations

The second factor influencing natural selection is the occurrence of what are called mutations. These are random changes which sometimes occur in the genes (that is, the DNA) of an individual living organism that produces a new characteristic not present in its parents but one that can be passed on to its offspring and to future generations. Although most mutations tend to be disadvantageous, some do make an individual better able to survive in the struggle for existence and to produce more offspring. An example is the mutation that occurred in mosquitoes that enabled them to resist insecticides, including the one known as DDT. When DDT was used on a large scale in an attempt to eliminate the insect-borne disease malaria, a mutation occurred which made some mosquitoes resistant to it. Those mosquitoes survived long enough to reproduce and they, and their resistant offspring, took over completely from the non-resistant insects that were wiped out: consequently malaria is still with us. The accumulation of many mutations over millions of years is believed to be the main way which evolution occurred. Darwin's theory, combined with modern knowledge of genetics, is now known as *neoDarwinism* ('new' Darwinism).

The evolution of complex organs

Many thinkers, including some scientists, have expressed doubts as to whether natural selection could explain the evolution of such complex structures as the higher animals. Darwin himself raised the question particularly in relation to the eye. The various tissues of the eye could not function properly in isolation: the transparent cornea at the front of the eye would be useless without the light-sensitive cells of the retina at the back of the eye which, in turn would be useless without nerves connecting it to the brain. It is inconceivable that all the necessary structures could arise from one mutation. However, two points make this easier to understand. It is now accepted that evolution of complicated structures like the eye occurred in many stages; some of these stages are still present in lowly creatures. A light-sensitive spot in a depression on the skin, such as still exists in leeches, might have developed first from a mutation. If the depression became larger and filled with jelly-like material (as the result of another mutation), as in some worms, it would act as a primitive lens and pigment added to the sensitive cells would introduce some colour vision. Thus it may be envisaged that these steps, each caused by a mutation and each being retained because they had survival value, could lead to the evolution of the eye as we know it. The second factor is that recent developments in biochemistry have established that DNA can be broken up, sometimes into quite large sections, which may be re-assembled in the cell nucleus in a different order. This leads to mutations and, when large sections are involved, to several mutations simultaneously.

It has been known for many years that the cells in the body – except the sex cells – contain all the genes necessary for producing all the bodily tissues so that in any one cell most genes do not exert their effect. For example, of all the genes in a skin cell, only those genes responsible for skin are 'switched on', the rest are made inactive by other substances (themselves genes) in the cell. This means that mutations may arise in two ways: by changes in the structure of the genes themselves and by changes in the extent to which they are switched on.

The role of chance in evolution

A criticism often heard of the theory of natural selection is that people 'can't believe that the human body evolved by chance'. It is true that mutations occur by chance but they are passed on to future generations only if the individual with the mutation lives long enough to have offspring. If the mutation allows them to be 'fitter', that is, live longer and have more offspring than individuals without the mutation, then the mutation is more likely to become established. In this way, the *effects* of the mutation, unlike the mutation itself, are not a matter of chance but influence evolution only if they increase the ability of the individual to pass on the mutation to future generations.

Is there a design and purpose in evolution?

One of the classical arguments for the existence of divine influence is based on the appearance of design in living things. Nobody with even the slightest knowledge of the panorama of nature can fail to be impressed by the way plants and animals fit into their environment. The lightweight build of birds, the streamlined shape of fish, as well as points of detail such as the webbed feet of waterbirds and the sharp teeth of flesh-eating animals are only a very few examples of what has been interpreted as evidence of special design. The theory of evolution by natural selection puts this argument into reverse. As living things diversified, as a result of natural variations or mutations, unless their shape and mode of living fitted their environment they simply did not survive. The beautiful adaptations shown by plants and animals exist because any other species that failed to develop these adaptations could not compete and became extinct. (*Another aspect of the argument from design is discussed on pages 85-6.*)

Some have argued that the process of evolution reveals a design and purpose in living things such as the purpose of becoming ever fitter to survive and to enjoy the world's resources. If there is evidence of design, it is argued that God was the designer. However, although evolution has shown a tendency towards increased complexity and fitness this has not always been so. Many species have become extinct without leaving any successors, others have undergone a change towards earlier forms, such as birds that have lost the ability to fly and mammals that have returned to the sea (whence early life came) to evolve into seals and whales. Also, in spite of the almost incredible efficiency of living things, too many features look like errors of design to suggest an intelligent creator. The Russian biologist Metchnikoff listed one hundred and twenty 'design faults' in the human body that might have been avoided if it had been designed by a team of engineers. One example is the complications, without any obvious advantages, arising from the fact that in the higher animals the millions of nerve fibres leaving each side of the brain cross over to control the opposite side of the body. Furthermore, it would not seem that a good designer, much less a loving one, would ever arrange that so many species of animals can survive only by the merciless killing and eating of other species. The existence of herbivorous animals and vegetarian human beings shows that flesh-eating is not a necessity for life.

In spite of the gaps in our knowledge, Humanists accept the scientific view that evolution by natural selection is the most likely hypothesis to explain how living things, including humankind, came into being. The possible influence of additional, largely unknown, factors cannot be dismissed, however. Humanists also think that the idea of evolution can be applied to the development of human society and its moral principles (*see Question 11*).

The fossil record shows that during the last 600 million years of evolution Earth has suffered five major catastrophes (*see pages 25-6*). The most recent occurred 65 million years ago and resulted in the extinction of the dinosaurs, until then the dominant species, and between 50 and 75% of other existing species. It is widely believed that this catastrophe arose from a collision between Earth and a minor planet which would cause very widespread fires and raise clouds of millions of tons of dust and rock that would black out the sun and disastrously reduce plant growth.

These impacts, possibly coinciding with the eruption of a supervolcano, (*see page 25*), had a profound effect on evolution, preventing any further evolution of dinosaurs. Among the few species of animal remaining were the early mammals, mouse-like creatures that lived in burrows and which could find enough food to meet their requirements until plant life recovered. In the absence of serious rivals, they survived and continued their evolution into the thousands of mammalian species that eventually formed. If these early mammals had not survived, later mammals – including the human race – would never have evolved!

Whilst many details are still unclear, the evidence is overwhelming and these ideas are now widely accepted. Only creationists, who base their beliefs on the account of creation in the Old Testament, think that the different species of living things were separately created, and have not evolved since their creation. They do not accept the massive evidence for evolution and give undue emphasis to the gaps in our knowledge and to any facts that are difficult to explain in evolutionary terms, such as the imperfections of the fossil records.

Further reading
Charles Darwin *The Origin of Species*
(Penguin edition, 1993)
Davies, Paul *The Fifth Miracle*
(Allen Lane, Penguin, 1998)

Dawkins, Richard *Climbing Mount Improbable*
(Penguin 1997)
Dawkins, Richard *The Blind Watchmaker*
(Longmans, 1986)
Dawkins, Richard *The Selfish Gene*
(2nd edition, Oxford University Press, 1989)
(*Other books by Dawkins are also relevant to this chapter*).
Miller, John and van Loon, B *Darwinism for Beginners*
(Icon Books, 1993)

9 MIND AND SOUL

Even if the theory of evolution can account for plants and animals, can it account for the mind and soul? Are not these different from matter?

ALTHOUGH IT IS OBVIOUS that the human body is a material object made of atoms and molecules like everything else in the universe, many people still think that the material body is in some way dominated by non-material entities of the mind, the will and the soul – a belief known as dualism. The expression 'victory of mind over matter' is sometimes heard meaning that the mind is supreme in forcing the body to undertake some activity. The terms mind, will and soul are used rather indiscriminately to refer to these entities but the words mind and soul really refer to different ideas.

The mind

The dominance of the human species over the earth has occurred because of the large size of the human brain (cerebrum), especially the outer layer, the *cerebral cortex* which controls intelligence and reasoning. The cortex is about 4 mm thick, much thicker than in the lower animals, and is made larger in area by being folded. The cortex of a human adult contains many billions of cells and each cell has innumerable connections with other brain cells so that the number and complexity of the 'circuits' through which nerve impulses may pass is enormous. This immense complexity makes it possible for human beings to be conscious, that is, aware of their own existence and of their surroundings (a process that is still completely unexplained). This complexity also enables information received through the senses to be stored in the memory and to be processed as imagination and original thought. These activities of the brain are called 'mind' but the use of this word should not imply that the mind has an existence independent of the body (contrary to earlier beliefs). It is obvious that the mind can affect the body. An enthusiasm for life can hasten recovery from illness and a competitive spirit can raise the physical stamina. There is also a close correlation between the condition of the body and the activity of the brain making it difficult to believe that the mind has a separate existence from the body. As the body grows in childhood so does the mind; when the body is fatigued, diseased or under the influence of drugs the mind is often affected in a similar way. Finally, as the body degenerates in old age, so usually does the mind. These considerations suggest that when the body dies, the mind dies with it.

The soul

In contrast to the mind, the idea of the soul is a religious concept for which there is no precise, agreed definition. It is usually taken to refer to an immaterial element which is the seat of the moral attributes of a person. Religious leaders have differed greatly in their teaching about the soul; some believe that the soul is in some way superior to the body while others believe that both are equal and work together in harmony. It is widely conceded by all except creationalists (*see page 81*) that the human body evolved from the lower animals, as Darwin suggested, but some religious leaders still think that only human beings have souls, given to them by God. All religious leaders agree that the soul survives death and some think it is immortal. *(The idea of reincarnation is discussed in Question 19.)* The extensive studies of psychology, neurology and psychiatry have produced no evidence for the existence of the soul. The idea is ignored by scientists. Humanists share this sceptical view and regard the soul as a figment of the theological imagination, depending on faith alone.

Further reading
Elbert J.W. *Does the Soul Exist?* in *Science and Religion* ed Paul Kurtz *(Prometheus Books 2003)*
Ryle, Gilbert *The Concept of the Mind*
(Hutchinson 1949, with many reprints by Penguin Books)

10 THE HUMANIST BASIS FOR MORALS
How do Humanists decide what is morally right and what is wrong?

FIRST, IT MAY BE OF INTEREST to clarify the meaning of the two words *morals* and *ethics*, as they are often loosely used interchangeably.

Morals (from the Latin) refers to a set of rules about right and wrong behaviour (sometimes incorrectly thought to refer only to sexual behaviour). *Ethics* (from the Greek) is not a list of rules, but a branch of philosophy concerned with a critical analysis of different views on the nature and basis of right and wrong throughout the course of history.

In those parts of the world where Judaism, Christianity and Islam have been dominant, the assumption has been that everything was determined by God who was thought to be all-powerful, all-good and all-wise. People had therefore a duty to learn the will of God and obey it. What helped a person to understand and obey the will of God was good. What hindered the understanding and obeying the will of God was bad. This has led to great conflicts because the will of God was (and still is) interpreted differently by different sects and even by different priests and other leaders within each sect. Many of the bloodiest wars in history have been fought over such questions.

A possible starting point for the Humanist approach to morals is the proposition that human wellbeing is preferable to human misery. The word *wellbeing* is more appropriate than *happiness* (the word used by the Utilitarians, *see next page*), as this is the same for everybody (the provision of adequate food, reasonable housing, good health and education for the full development of personality). Happiness, on the other hand, is a very personal thing. The preference for wellbeing rather than misery is a value judgement and cannot therefore be proved right or wrong but is surely accepted by all reasonable people. The Humanist criterion for a good or bad action is the effect of that action on human wellbeing. Those actions that improve wellbeing or decrease human misery are good whereas those actions that reduce wellbeing and increase misery are bad (as John Stuart Mill proposed in 1863). If an action has no effect on human wellbeing then it can be regarded as morally neutral and it does not matter whether it is undertaken or not.

Thus Humanist morals can be considered to be based on the Utilitarian principle (*see page 6*) of the 'greatest happiness for the greatest number' with *happiness* being replaced by *wellbeing*.

Comparison of ethical strategies by computer games

In recent decades computer games or *tournaments* have been devised by social scientists in which various ethical strategies have been played against each other in an attempt to decide their relative merits. One social scientist advertised, inviting colleagues to participate by submitting strategies: over 60 replies were received and as a result a very large number of confrontations were carried out.

There is no space for a full account of the games here, but for details of the procedures and results of some of the strategies see Dawkins, *The Selfish Gene* and Babcock, *Evolution and Individual Behaviour.*

These strategies were given nicknames, such as *Tit-for-tat, Tat-for-tit, Tit-for-two-tats, Random, Sucker, Tester* and *Tranquilliser. Tit* represented a good turn (co-operation) and *Tat* a dirty trick (defection). Each move of the game scored or lost a point, giving a total for the whole game. Eventually the scores of all the games were compared. The strategy which gained the highest score was *Tit-for-tat* – which meant starting with co-operation, then copying the moves of the opponent, which for this strategy means repeating the co-operation. Its success depends largely on the opening move of co-operation, which encourages the opponent to do likewise.

It must be emphasised that in this terminology *Tit-for-tat* does not represent the revengeful Old Testament rule of an eye for an eye and a tooth for a tooth (which would be *Tat-for-tit* and is unacceptable to Humanists). *Tit-for-tat* agrees with the idea of reciprocal altruism mentioned on page 64.

A question that arises is, How can altruism develop from natural selection, involving competition ('nature red in tooth and claw')? One suggested answer is summarised by Babcock: 'Altruism can evolve if altruists benefit other altruists but do not benefit non-altruists'.

How should Humanists deal with people whose behaviour invites disapproval? A suggestion is to ostracise them, and possibly any associates who share their unacceptable views, and this may give the message without involving any dirty tricks.

Tit-for-tat as an ethical guide can be summarised as 'trying to be a good neighbour' and living by the Golden Rule which has been a guide to good conduct for 2500 years (*See page 6*). In the form given by Confucius – 'Do not do to others what you would not like them to do to you' – the rule is negative and merely an instruction not to be hurtful to people. The Jewish form 'Love thy neighbour as thyself' and the Christian form 'Do unto others as you would have them do to you' clearly suggest acts of kindliness and good neighbourliness on a reciprocal basis. Although George Bernard Shaw's contradiction of the Rule ('Don't do unto others as you would have them do to you – their tastes might be different!') is too dogmatic, it does suggest it would be prudent to consider other people's likes and dislikes before applying the Rule.

Although in practice some moral principles of Christianity and Humanism are very similar, the reasons for adopting them are very different. Christians try to follow the rule because it is God's will, as taught by Christ. Humanists adopt the rule because it is built into their conscience, they think it is a product of evolution (*see Question 11*) and furthers their aim of raising the level of human wellbeing.

In addition to friendly personal contacts many Humanists feel the urge to act in a wider field. This can be achieved by joining and working for charitable bodies, pressure groups and political parties in one's own community.

The global village

Humanists also think that, in these days of rapid transport and with television coverage of world events in almost every home, the whole world has to be regarded as a neighbour. Actions taken in one area can influence people far away. For example, high interest rates in a rich western country may prevent a poor third world country from borrowing to provide much needed development. Humanists feel impelled to support anti-racist movements and to help to build up an internationally-minded public opinion. This can be done by writing letters to the press or to MPs and, in some cases, writing articles or books, giving talks or raising funds. There is no shortage of ways to help. Humanists are encouraged to take an interest in world affairs as this puts them in a better position to decide which movements or charities are likely to be most effective in improving human well-being generally.

How can Humanists be sure about the effect of their actions?

One problem that greatly concerns Humanists is: How do they decide the effects of their actions and how can they be sure that what they think improves wellbeing does in fact do so? For example, should a street of well-kept houses be demolished to make way for a motorway that will reduce accidents and traffic jams? In a democracy, a finely balanced question like this can be investigated by public enquiries and local attitudes can be judged by conducting opinion polls. Admittedly, enquiries are often prejudiced and public opinion is often emotional and ill-informed but enquiries do help the process of discussion and debate. These procedures can be expected to become more effective with improved education and as more experience is gained. A decision can then be taken in accordance with majority opinion with generous compensation for the minority who are compelled to make sacrifices.

Another example of the difficulty in applying the Utilitarian principle of increasing the general level of human well-being is as follows. Is it wrong for poverty-stricken parents to steal food from a supermarket to feed their hungry children? The increased well-being from feeding the children is greater than the negligible effect of the loss by the supermarket. However, this act breaks the rule – upon which the smooth running of society depends – that stealing is wrong. Most humanists believe in obeying the law unconditionally (although some might think it justifiable to break minor laws if this publicises or promotes some larger issue) and would therefore disapprove of this act. They would use their energy and whatever influence they have to help build a society in which there was no poverty. This, however, is a long-term solution; in the short term, Humanists would consider this a case of extenuating circumstances and would probably favour lenient punishment.

When it comes to wider issues of conflict between nations, the morally fair solution is more difficult. Traditionally nations have settled conflicts by war. Although the United Nations constitutes, for the first time in history, a body supported by almost every country in the world and although able to discuss disputes and suggest solutions, it is not strong enough to enforce its advice. Hence Humanists have a clear aim to work for the spreading of democracy and human rights and the strengthening of the United Nations to increase its authority.

The working compromise

In many situations, even after exhaustive analysis and discussion, the parties to a dispute cannot agree on a definite conclusion. In cases like this, that may occur at the personal, national and international level, Humanists advocate the principle of agreeing to a 'working compromise': an agreement to differ on some issues but still allowing a working relationship. The compromise may often be temporary and if it breaks down another compromise will have to be negotiated and this may lead to a more permanent solution.

The fallibility of all ethical systems

It must be admitted that Humanists sometimes do have difficulty in deciding what action is likely to be most successful in raising the quality of human life. However, the adherents of theistic religions have similar difficulties as they are rarely able to agree what is the will of God and how it should be implemented. A study of the many ethical systems proposed over the centuries shows that none of them is free from criticism and difficulties. Humanists think that their view-point of morality – the effect of a decision on human well-being – is sensible, easier to understand and no more difficult to apply than other moral criteria. In spite of differences in outlook, the Humanist movement is, of course, willing to co-operate with Christians and the supporters of other religions and beliefs in the search for, and the implementation of, agreed policies and activities for promoting human wellbeing.

While the welfare of human beings is the main concern of Humanists it is realised that this should not be at the expense of animals. The higher animals can feel pain and show clear signs of suffering emotional stress. Animals have been (and still are) subjected to appalling cruelty as sources of food, in performing work, as sporting objects and even as pets. Without being sentimental or unreasonable many Humanists would include the welfare of animals in their moral code.

Why are Humanists concerned about others?

A further question that arises is, why should Humanists be concerned about the welfare of others especially when this involves a sacrifice of time, money or convenience? The Humanist answer is that, as mentioned above, some measure of altruism is built into all human personalities (it is well-known that there is even 'honour among thieves'). We assume that others, like ourselves, do not like to suffer pain and therefore it gives us pain to see others impoverished or hurt. In our dealings with others, it pays us to be fair, just and honest, hoping that they will be the same with us.

We have at present no power to modify genetic influences on behaviour. This may become possible in the future with advances in genetic engineering although it is doubtful whether it would ever be desirable. Society is based on the assumption that we have control over environmental factors that affect moral behaviour, such as education and parental example (*but see Question 17*). Education and parental influence and the type of government can enhance altruism and discourage selfishness. Humanists can use their votes and personal influence to encourage those who are altruistic and restrain those who are selfish.

Postmodernism

In conclusion, some mention should be made of the philosophical and cultural movements known as *Modernism* and *Postmodernism*.

Modernism was widely held during the 1920s, and believed in the existence and accessibility of objective truth and accepted that scientific method was the only valid means of establishing facts – clearly the theme of this book.

Postmodernism, current since the 1950s, and a reaction against Modernism, asserts that there is no objective truth. Rationality is said to depend on one's 'perspective'. It suggests that scientific method is one such perspective among others (but Humanists would find it difficult to know what the 'others' are!). This reaction against Modernism leads to *Relativism*, including *Ethical relativism*: the doctrine that ethical statements may be may be true for one group of people but false for another group. Humanists would strongly disagree with this bleak and negative attitude as it would undermine their aim of upgrading the general level of human wellbeing.

The Humanist ethical approach to some practical issues

Stem cells

It is obvious that a fertilised ovum contains the potential for producing all the specialised cells in the body. The first development of the fertilised ovum is the production of the pre-embryo which contains 'stem cells' and these can also, in suitable environments, develop into specialised cells. It has been suggested that diseases caused by the loss or malfunctioning of cells such as Parkinson's and Alzheimer's, diabetes and heart disease, might be treated by injecting stem cells into the afflicted organ. In this environment the stems cells become converted into the specialised cells required for recovery.

The simplest method of acquiring the necessary pre-embryo is by in vitro fertilisation (IVF) in which an ovum is collected by medical personnel and mixed with sperm in a glass vessel. When the ovum becomes fertilised it forms a pre-embryo which contains stem cells.

Alternatively, pre-embryos can be created by artificial insemination in which the sperm is injected into the woman's uterus so that fertilisation takes place in the normal environment. The pre-embryo, a bunch of cells scarcely visible to the naked eye, is removed by medical personnel and its stem cells collected.

In Britain after the stem cells are removed the surviving tissue of the pre-embryo must be destroyed by law within 14 days. Some religious people object to this activity, believing that the pre-embryo already contains a soul and that its destruction would therefore be sinful (that is, contrary to the will of God). In America and most other countries all stem cell research is prohibited, preventing the possibility of using this technique therapeutically. Humanists take the view that stem cell research has great potential in medicine, as well as in pure research into cellular development, and far from being prohibited should be encouraged.

Stem cells exist also in the adult bone marrow but their extraction from this source is not easy – although their use clearly avoids the religious objections to embryonic stem cells. Some of the earlier results of marrow stem cells injected into a blood vessel leading to the heart seemed spectacular, but have not been consistently confirmed. The stem cell research is still at an early stage and much more work is needed on the factors which control the development of stem cells into specialised tissues. Nevertheless, some trials in large groups of patients are being planned both in Europe and the UK.

Sex education and contraception

Humanists recognise that early sexual activity does occur and efforts should be made to reduce any avoidable social consequences. Humanists believe that knowledge of, and access to, effective means of contraception and health advice should be made freely available. Humanists believe there is a need to instill a responsible attitude to sexual matters without guilt.

Marriage

Humanists recognise marriage as a valuable institution but, of course, without any religious significance. They also accept that many couples are happy living together without the commitment of marriage. Whilst for years registry office weddings were seen as by many as greatly inferior to a 'real wedding in a church', the restrictions surrounding civil ceremonies have recently been relaxed so events may now be held in many different locations and Humanist ceremonies are becoming increasingly common.

Divorce may be an appropriate solution to certain situations to avoid a greater hurt; the former social disapproval is no longer an issue.

Homosexuality

It is estimated that between 5% and 10% of the population have a natural preference for close relations with members of their own sex; homosexuality among animals also has been well documented. Arising from Jewish laws laid down (twice) in Leviticus, homosexual acts were punishable by death: Henry VIII introduced a similar law in England that was not repealed until 1861, when the maximum punishment was reduced to life imprisonment.

The causes of homosexuality are still uncertain. Twin studies imply a genetic influence and recent research (not yet fully established) has associated it with a modified gene probably causing small differences in brain structure. Whatever the cause, sexual orientation is outside the control of the individual. Humanists would wish to combat the prejudice against homosexuality which still exists, despite decriminalisation of homosexual acts in 1967.

Recent studies have shown that homosexual men tend to have more elder brothers than heterosexual men. The probability of a man being homosexual rises by one third for each elder brother. The explanation is not known but one suggestion is that male foetuses affect a mother's immune system in such a way that her uterus may alter the sexual orientation of boys born later.

The importance of this finding is that it is increased evidence that sexual orientation is decided biologically and is not a lifestyle choice.

Abortion

The religious objections to abortion are based on the already-mentioned belief that even a fertilised ovum possesses a soul and is a human person and that to destroy it is murder. Humanists take the more realistic view that until the nervous system is sufficiently developed to sustain consciousness and the foetus is viable (that is, would survive in the event of a premature birth) it cannot be regarded as having rights as a human being. The existing law accepts that the foetus becomes viable at about 26 weeks after fertilisation, but even at this stage the evidence from premature births shows that risk of abnormalities is high and the survival rate low.

Abortion should not be undertaken lightly but there are circumstances (for example, evidence of congenital disability or even a pregnant teenager with insufficient resources to look after a baby) in which the short term problems of an abortion are outweighed by the long term benefits.

Voluntary euthanasia

The religious objection to euthanasia (that God gave us life and only God should end it) obviously carries no weight with Humanists. The more practical objection which perhaps many people fear is that if euthanasia were lawful, their end might be accelerated by unscrupulous and impatient relatives who would benefit by their death.

At present it is illegal to assist anybody to die or even assist them to commit suicide. Occasionally relatives and compassionate doctors have risked prosecution because of their actions in helping someone die with dignity and without pain.

The Voluntary Euthanasia Society (address in appendix) exists to promote the idea of *voluntary* euthanasia whereby the patient's decision (and their right to possibly change their mind) is paramount. The VES has devised a document, called a Living Will, which aims at helping the participant choose what should happen if they later suffer from a condition which, in the opinion of two doctors, they are unlikely to recover. The document is signed while the participant is fit and well in the presence of two witnesses. The Living Will gives the participant two alternatives. The first choice is opting out, in which case they will continue to receive medical treatment to keep them alive. The second option (which is most appealing to those who believe in voluntary euthanasia) is that of refusing medical treatment aimed at prolonging life while consenting only to treatment aiming to keep them comfortable and hopefully free from pain.

Humanists would like to see the law changed so that the terminally ill can not only die with dignity and without pain, but with the option of requesting medical assistance to die. In October 2004 a bill was put forward to the House of Lords which would amend the present law and achieve this change. More than 100,000 people sent messages to the House of Lords select committee in support of this bill.

The activities of the VES, both in promoting the idea of the Living Will and lobbying for changes in the law, deserve to be more widely known (a recent survey showed that many people had never heard of either voluntary euthanasia or the VES).

Crime and punishment

The long-term (if perhaps Utopian) approach of Humanists is to determine and deal with the many causes of crime. Meanwhile, attempts must be made to control crime by direct and physical means including punishments given by the courts. The aims of punishment are the expression of society's disapproval, protection of the public, deterrence, reform and retribution. There is little precise information on the effects of different punishments or on how they affect different types of offenders. The current policy of increasing imprisonment only achieves an expression of society's disapproval and the protection of the public for a limited time only – and at considerable expense. Much more research on this subject is urgently needed.

It is known that anti-social behaviour runs in families and sometimes it is difficult to decide how much of this is genetic and how much occurs from following the example of other members of the family.

A particular difficulty arises with psychopaths (individuals often above normal intelligence and with a disarming charm who may suddenly become highly aggressive, even to the point of committing murder, after which they experience no feelings of guilt). Psychiatrists have emphasised the difficulty of diagnosing this condition and it is virtually impossible to predict whether a psychopath will offend again.

Capital punishment

Capital punishment is rejected by Humanists, because it is meeting violence with violence, miscarriages of justice cannot be rectified, it does not seem to be an effective deterrent (perhaps this is because most murders are unpremeditated) and it encourages an unhealthy, morbid curiosity (in the USA executions have been televised). Further, if juries know that a guilty verdict will lead to the death of the accused, they are more likely to acquit; some guilty murderers have not been convicted for this reason.

In cases of political assassination and bombings, capital punishment makes the criminals into martyrs and strengthens the resolve of their organisations.

Further reading
Babcock, Christopher   *Evolution and Individual Behaviour*
(Basil Blackwell 1991*)*
Barr, Chandler   *A Separate Creation: How biology makes us gay*
(Bantam, 1996)
Chapter 7 contains a detailed account of the discovery of the gene affecting homosexuality.
Dawkins, Richard   *The Selfish Gene*
(2nd edition, Oxford University Press, 1989)
Mill, John Stuart   *Utilitarianism* (First published 1863)
Warburton, Nigel   *Philosophy: The Basics* (Chapter 2)
(Routledge, 1995)
Ward, Glen   *Postmodernism*
(Hodder Headline 2003)
Warnock, Mary   *Making Babies*
(Oxford University Press, 2002)

THE ORIGIN OF MORALS

How do Humanists account for the origin of morals? Have not morals arisen from religious belief?

TODAY THERE ARE MANY PEOPLE who never go to a place of worship and either do not believe in any gods at all or have only a vague notion of a God but do not think that He has any influence over their everyday lives. These same people can be law-abiding citizens who get on well with their neighbours and play responsible parts in their communities. From a moral point of view they cannot be distinguished from devoutly religious people. It is clear that moral behaviour does not depend on having a religious faith, although many people do not seem to realise that there can be a basis for morals other than religion. A further illustration of the independence of morals from religion is that many books that deal with ethics in great depth (and often at excessive length!) either make no mention at all of religion, or mention religion only incidentally. So if morals do not necessarily arise from religion, where do they come from?

Evolutionary hypotheses of the origins of morals

Humanists think that morals are a product of evolution although the details of how this might have occurred are still controversial.

There is no doubt that altruism – the taking of risks or making of sacrifices for the benefit of others – exists among animals other than humankind. When predators are seen, alarm calls are often made by birds and mammals who draw attention to themselves (thereby increasing the risk of being caught) but give a warning enabling other members of the group to take evasive action. Assuming that animals have no religious sense, this suggests that moral behaviour has a biological, rather than a divine, origin.

Group selection

Darwin pointed out (in *The Descent of Man*) that, in the early social life of humankind, several individuals working together could undertake larger projects and acquire greater safety from the many hazards that confronted them than if they acted separately. For example, a group of hunters could catch more and larger animals for food and defend their homes more effectively against dangers such as floods or predators than could individuals acting singly. It seems reasonable to suppose that in the course of evolution people possessing genes that favour co-operation with others, who have altruistic ideas of living with the interests of others in mind, tend to have a better chance of survival. Thus, the argument runs, during the early development of human society, altruistic people will live longer and have the opportunity to have larger families. In this way, it is suggested, the urge to co-operate became built into the human personality.

Environmental factors might be expected to reinforce the effects of genes on altruism. Children brought up in an altruistic family would tend to regard friendly co-operation as the accepted pattern of behaviour (an example of the spread of what Dawkins has called *memes*, see page 101). On the other hand, children often oppose the views of their parents, especially in a rapidly developing society in which succeeding generations have widely differing opinions. (*See twin studies, page 64.*)

The idea that altruism developed because co-operative people survive better is called *group selection*. Although quite widely accepted, it has been criticised on two main grounds.

First, some evolutionists think that natural selection works only on individuals and not on groups. However, it might be expected that a mutation for altruism in an individual would, after several generations, lead to the birth of a sufficient number of people with the mutation for them to influence the group. In addition, the example set by those with the mutation would be expected to have some effect on the behaviour of the group, as mentioned above (*and later, see page 64*).

The second criticism of group selection is that sometimes selfish people, especially in an acquisitive society, become rich, influential and may even dominate the group. If it is assumed that altruism is inherited, then presumably selfishness is also inherited. This raises the possibility that selfish people would eventually outnumber the altruistic members of society – the opposite of what the group selection theory suggests. This can be answered by the observation that people acquire a mixture of selfish and altruistic traits in varying proportions (mostly by genetic factors) and this could explain the range of behaviour from the criminal to the saintly. In a mature society, an approximate equilibrium is eventually reached between these opposing groups. The position of the equilibrium obviously varies in different societies and at different times. Sometimes a Mafia-like criminal class or a ruthless dictator may be in control while, in a liberal democracy, the altruistic members may dominate and keep in check the selfish and criminal minority.

The selfish gene hypothesis

Another hypothesis to explain the origin of morals is based on what the zoologist Richard Dawkins has rather confusingly called (in his influential book with the same name) *the selfish gene*. This does not mean a gene that makes an individual selfish in the ordinary sense, but one that *makes people act in ways that favour the survival of their own genes*, some of which are, of course, shared with relatives. The continuation of many animal species (including humankind) depends on the willingness of parents to feed and care for their young and, to a lesser extent, for others with whom they have a close family relationship (kinship). In other words, their behaviour is such as to increase the chances of their children and relatives surviving and being in a position to pass on their genes to future generations. This idea was rather whimsically illustrated by a remark said to have been made in a pub by Professor J.B.S. Haldane

(1892 – 1964) the distinguished biochemist, mathematician and geneticist. Asked whether he would be prepared to die to save a brother he replied 'No, but I would for three brothers or nine cousins!' His point was that these two groups of relatives would be able to pass on more copies of his genes than would be lost if he had died (brothers share half of an individual's genes and cousins one eighth).

Kin selection and reciprocal altruism

Thus, it is suggested, altruism was originally limited to close family members but as societies evolved, it gradually extended to others. One suggested basis for the widening of altruism is that it occurred from reciprocating helpful acts. This is found even in animals who are often seen to help each other, for example, a pair of monkeys may take turns to groom each other. In an experiment to investigate the idea of 'reciprocal altruism' the cries for help from several monkeys were tape-recorded When the calls were played back, the monkeys responded most vigorously to the calls from those monkeys that had previously groomed them.

On present knowledge, it is not yet possible to choose between these hypotheses that attempt to explain the development of altruism in the course of human evolution. The important point is that there are these several ideas that give plausible explanations for altruism and it is not necessary to assume that it arose from divine revelation or that it requires a belief in God.

Twin studies

One way of trying to measure the relative importance of nature (genes) and nurture (environmental effect) is by the study of identical twins. Unlike fraternal twins, caused by the fertilisation of two ova which happen to have been released from the ovary at the same time and are no more alike than non-twinned siblings, identical twins arise because a fertilised ovum divides, forming two embryos with identical genes. Sir Francis Galton, a half-cousin of Charles Darwin pioneered in 1869 the study of twins by comparing their similarities and differences. He found that the identical twins resembled each other in appearance, health and personality, much more closely than did fraternal twins.

Unfortunately, by 1970 the idea of twin studies had became discredited partly because it had been abused by the Nazis who were trying to substantiate the idea of a master race, and partly by the dishonest reporting of twin studies by an English educationalist Sir Cyril Burt. Twin studies were resumed in 1979 by Thomas Bouchard. He studied first, a pair of identical twins who had been separated by adoption when a few weeks old but were not reunited until the age of 40. He found their appearance, medical histories, interests and hobbies were extremely similar. Massive publicity of this study led to contact with 39 pairs of identical twins and a similar number of fraternal twins who were prepared to be put through a battery of tests: the results confirmed the importance of genes. As an extension to this work, Bouchard then studied identical and fraternal twins who had been reared apart, also confirming previous results. By the use of questionnaires it was shown that even religious and political views were 69% correlated in the identical twins with no correlation at all in the fraternal twins.

These twin studies suggest that genes are far more important than environment in moulding personality – an idea that may surprise and dismay some parents. But it is widely accepted that a happy family does have an influence, although this does not seem to have been adequately investigated by quantitative studies. Such an investigation would be difficult to carry out: how could researchers tactfully collect comparable groups, some with and others without, a happy family environment?

Twin studies and intelligence

Unlike personality, the intelligence quotient (IQ) has been found in identical twins to be influenced both by genes and environmental factors such as the socio-economic level of the family. One estimate suggests that the IQ is affected approximately 50% by genes and 25% by shared environment, and 25% by individual environmental factors such as illness or accidents.

No genes have been discovered which seem to be associated with general intelligence, but a correlation has been found (much higher in identical than fraternal twins) between the IQ and the amount of grey matter (the brain cells) in certain parts of the brain, suggesting that the number of brain cells is correlated with intelligence. (For a fuller discussion of twin studies, see Matt Ridley: *Nature via Nurture*).

The present-day evolution of morals

The evolution of morals is continuing to this day. As the environment changes and knowledge increases so moral attitudes and the laws based on them change. This can lead to conflict in society. Attitudes to divorce, family planning, abortion, race and armaments are very different today from what they were a few decades ago and these changes are not welcomed by all. Another example is the growing realisation that the earth's environment is a delicate ecological balance which requires world-wide co-operation for its protection for both present and future generations.

Some experiments have suggested that amongst environmental factors, the provision of a dietary supplement of minerals and vitamins can raise the level of academic achievement and reduce disruptive behaviour. The results of these experiments are still in dispute but it seems unlikely that these supplements would benefit children on a varied well-balanced diet, but might affect those receiving a diet deficient in these substances.

Further Reading
Darwin, Charles   *The Descent of Man*
(first published 1871)
Dawkins, Richard   *The Selfish Gene*
(Oxford University Press, 1989)

Gribbin, Mary and John *Being Human (Chapters 7 and 9)*
(Phoenix, 1993)
Ridley, Matt *Nature Via Nurture*
(Fourth Estate, 2003)
and *The Origins of Virtue*
(Viking, 1996)
de Waal, Frans *Good Natured: The Origins of Right and Wrong in Humans and Other Animals*
(Harvard University Press, 1996)
Warburton, Nigel *Philosophy: The Basics* (Chapter 2)

12 CONSCIENCE
What is the Humanist attitude to conscience?

THE TRADITIONAL CHRISTIAN BELIEF about conscience is that it acted like a receiving apparatus, a sort of inner ear, for the reception of divinely inspired messages that give guidance on moral problems. Humanists naturally reject this view and think that conscience arises from living in a community and from being brought up to observe its laws and customs.

In any community there is a centre of authority. In a family with a young baby the parents make the decisions concerning the baby's welfare. From the first beginnings of awareness the baby realises that the parents are the source of comfort, food, warmth and cleanliness. The baby soon becomes aware that there are ways of behaving which the parents regard as good or bad. If the baby behaves well and pleases the parents it learns that it will be rewarded with cuddles, kisses and smiles. If it behaves badly it learns to expect disapproving words and gestures and possibly some form of punishment. The baby becomes a child and is made to feel pleased with itself if its behaviour meets with the approval of its parents. On the other hand if its behaviour is disapproved of the parents' reaction will give it a guilty feeling. There is therefore usually instilled into the child's mind (including the subconscious) a sense of the parents' attitude to right and wrong. This feeling of guilt or of self-satisfaction is what is meant by conscience.

As children grow up and come into contact with a wider community they find that some customs have been given the force of law, the aim of which is to maintain a stable society. If the laws are not obeyed, society may exact a punishment, thus reinforcing and extending the sense of right and wrong.

However, people do not always observe the moral codes and may sometimes break the law. How can their conscience allow this to happen? There are three main reasons for this. First, temptations arising from greed, jealousy, selfishness or arrogance may be too great for the conscience to control. Secondly, some people may never have been taught the difference between right and wrong or given a basis upon which they could make their own distinctions between right and wrong. Thirdly, many people regard some customs or laws as being out-of-date and therefore they suffer little in the way of a guilty conscience when they fail to observe them.

Ideally in a democracy all laws should be based on consent but sometimes laws are kept on the statute book long after most people have withdrawn their consent. Consequently they have a clear conscience in disobeying laws which they regard as undemocratic.

Changing standards of right and wrong

Environmental, cultural and educational conditions change and this leads to changes in customs and laws. Actions and attitudes which were once regarded as widely accepted are today seriously questioned – for example, slavery, child labour and colonial wars. The pendulum can also swing the other way, and behaviour formerly viewed with disapproval may become widely accepted. Divorce and contraception were disapproved of by the vast majority of people a century ago and abortion was illegal in Britain until quite recently. Today, in a more liberal society these are widely accepted and with the exception of abortion cause few qualms of conscience.

Humanists would wish to encourage more research into the causes of crime so that the relative importance of the above and any other factors can be assessed. The prevention of crime can be undertaken rationally only if there is more evidence about its causes. It is self-evident that the present methods of dealing with crime are largely ineffective.

In recent decades a great deal of crime (one estimate suggests as much as 70%) is drug-related. Addicts need money to buy their drugs and often they can only acquire enough by dishonest means. Smuggling of drugs and subsequent laundering of the massive proceeds lead to other crimes.

The internationality of conscience

While a change in morals is taking place there is inevitably a state of conflict in society. The scope of conflict has steadily widened. In early times conflicts would be within or between families. The formation of tribes and nations required new customs and laws as each group became larger. Today, we are realising more and more that nations are interdependent. Groups of nations are linking together for cooperative action, such as the European Union and the Organisation for African Unity. Customs and laws appropriate to the individual nation may become inappropriate when the nation becomes a member of a group.

Thus while the meaning of conscience remains the same (a feeling of satisfaction or guilt from obeying or disobeying customs and laws that protect the community) the scope of conscience has steadily widened. The human conscience now has to wrestle with questions affecting not only the welfare of groups of nations but of the whole world.

13 SCIENCE AND RESPONSIBILITY

Humanism seems to put its trust in science, but are not many of the world's problems, such as the pollution of air, water and food, the controversial effects of GM food, and the development of nuclear weapons, the direct responsibility of scientists? What can we do as individuals to check these problems?

SCIENTIFIC DISCOVERIES over the last few hundred years have paved the way for new technologies and the development of a society based on industry rather than agriculture. Many safeguards we now have come to expect were hard won and only came about because of unexpected calamities and disasters. Health and safety regulations, while irksome to many, were introduced by scientists in order that the workforce and the public are not exposed to unnecessary dangers.

Pesticides and fertilisers

It is, of course, obvious that scientists were responsible for finding out experimentally which substances would act as pesticides and fertilisers and this was done in order to increase food production. Later, perhaps from the use of larger quantities than were really necessary, it began to be realised that potentially harmful residues of pesticides entered foods and that fertilisers (especially nitrates) seeped into some water supplies at undesirably high concentrations. This is now well-known and pressure of public opinion is forcing governments to restrict their use. Farmers, using information provided by scientists, were therefore inadvertently responsible for this pollution.

Food additives

Food additives are used for a variety of reasons. Some (for example vitamins C and B_1, and the minerals calcium and iron) increase the nutritive value of the foods to which they are added.

Other additives improve appearance, intensify flavour or lengthen the shelf-life. In other words, while some additives are beneficial to the consumer others are mainly for the profit of industry or the shopkeeper. While scientists in the food industry were responsible for suggesting which substances might be used, other scientists have since shown that some additives could be harmful, at least to some sensitive people. Whether the amounts used in food reach undesirable levels is a very controversial question.

In most developed countries there are official bodies who monitor and control the permitted levels of additives on the advice of yet more scientists. Clearly, the responsibility is divided among several groups, of which scientists are only one and their contributions are mostly technical and advisory, rather than decision-making.

Genetically modified foods

Experiments have shown that it is not difficult for skilled staff in a well-equipped laboratory to isolate genes from the chromosomes of one organism and insert them into the cells of other organisms – which is the basis of GM foods. The value and safety of this development has become a highly controversial subject, with entrenched views on both sides. The original hopes were that GM crops would have high yields and could make a substantial contribution to the food supplies of developing countries, and political and commercial statements have been made that this has already occurred. A counter-claim is that GM seeds are not being produced for the basic cereals – wheat, rice and maize – as it is easier to improve their yields by crossing with related grasses by conventional means and that they have already been improved during the 'green revolution' of the 1960s and 70s (*see page 107*). It is stated that only profitable commercial crops of soya, rapeseed and tomatoes have used GM techniques and that research has been dominated by big companies, which some critics suggest are the main beneficiaries of GM foods.

Fears have been expressed about the safety of GM food crops. It is argued that unnatural genes might reduce their nutritional value and even cause the production of poisons. It has been stated that a few isolated tests of GM foods have shown toxic reactions but none has been followed up. The British Medical Association has stated that 'there has not yet been a robust and thorough search for potentially harmful effects'. In USA, hundreds of millions of people have been eating GM foods for a decade with no reports of any harm but minor complaints may have occurred, and without thorough medical vigilance might not have been detected.

One experiment on GM potatoes fed to rats led to thickening of the lining of the stomach and intestines. But this was not investigated further and the scientist who did the work retired (one press report stated he was 'hounded out of his job'). In China, GM rice was produced containing carotene, the precursor of vitamin A, which could be extremely beneficial to the many thousands who are showing symptoms of vitamin A deficiency. Its importance was belittled by pointing out that many vegetables contain vitamin A and therefore including it in rice is unnecessary.

With such contradictory reports the effectiveness and safety of GM foods must still be regarded as uncertain. Some GM crops are produced to be herbicide-tolerant, enabling farmers to use higher levels of herbicides to deal with weeds without it affecting the crop, but a possible danger is that the higher levels used might damage wild-life. Another possibility is that seeds from GM crops might spread to neighbouring fields and lead to the production of 'super-weeds'. A large-scale experiment (said to be the largest survey of farm ecology in the world) to test these possibilities was carried out in Britain between 1999 and 2003. Three GM crops were used and the result was that two of them did have greater effects on plant and insect life than normal crops and the third was more protective for wild-life than conventional crops.

Industrial pollution

Many industrial processes create products on which society depends, but unfortunately involve the production of unpleasant and dangerous by-products which enter the environment. Coal-burning power stations produce sulphur-containing smoke that helps to form acid rain. Despite the removal of lead from petrol, the engines of cars pollute the atmosphere with carbon monoxide. Nuclear power stations – the so-called clean option – create waste products that remain dangerously radioactive. Safeguarding this waste is an obligation we are imposing on our successors, in some cases for many centuries.

Scientists have worked out methods of avoiding or dealing with most of these problems but their application is very expensive. It has to be realised that the price of many goods would rise substantially if manufacturers adopted the complicated precautions necessary to make industry pollution-free. Although much improvement has been made in recent years – largely in response to public demand – a tighter control of pollution would require both the introduction and vigorous enforcement of legislation limiting or stopping the release of toxic wastes. Sadly, it seems no government is prepared to take these drastic actions.

So what are the alternatives to accepting the high cost of reducing pollution? One obvious but unlikely option is a return to more primitive technologies. Next is the development of new methods of manufacture and energy production that do not cause pollution. Windmills, solar panels and tidal power could be used to generate electricity but whether on a scale to meet modern energy requirements is uncertain. Their development would also be expensive and take many years to complete. While nuclear power prevents many forms of pollution it raises the more serious and still unsolved problem of storing nuclear waste.

The effect of industry on the environment has been obvious for generations but was tolerated by the public, and the industrialists who were directly responsible regarded it as merely a nuisance and inconvenience, rather than a menace to health and wellbeing. Only recently have the disastrous effects been fully realised of acid rain, water pollution and the release into the atmosphere of substances contributing to the greenhouse effect. Fortunately, public opinion is now fully aware of the problem and pressure on governments and industry is beginning to show results. Again responsibility is divided; industrialists, politicians, scientists and the general public – the consumers – all must share the blame.

Nuclear and chemical weapons

The decision to develop and stockpile nuclear and chemical weapons was a political one based on the belief that they preserve the international peace. It is the fear, real or imaginary, of potential aggression that leads to majority support for the defence policies involving these weapons. The scientists who invented nuclear weapons during the second world war realised that the survival of democracy depended on the production of an atomic weapon before the totalitarian powers produced one, although many scientists were aware of the horrendous implications of nuclear weapons and worked with an uneasy conscience. The decision after the war to produce the even more powerful hydrogen bomb was a political one aimed at deterring further aggression that was feared in the Cold War atmosphere at the time.

The use of chemical weapons has a long history. The ancient Greeks are said to have used sulphur fumes to poison and choke their enemies. 'Greek fire', a combustible mixture of uncertain composition, was used to destroy enemy ships in the seventh century BCE. Evidently military men exploited early scientific knowledge for use in weapons – a practice that has continued to the present day. However much this may be regretted (and surely Humanists regret this very strongly) it would seem that for as long as there is an armaments industry, some of the vast array of scientific knowledge will be applied to weaponry. Governments (including democratic governments and therefore the public), share the responsibility for this use of science in the name of defence.

The role of democracy

The decisions about how to apply scientific knowledge are made by politicians, industrialists and financiers. In a democracy there is an elaborate system by which many people vote to elect politicians. Thus, ultimately the voters are collectively responsible for what politicians do. Unfortunately, policies that involve the side effects of applied science are seldom election issues and political parties may have general programmes which gain the approval of the majority of voters but also carry out policies involving environmental damage. Politicians have to rely on information supplied by experts who may fail to point out (or even may not have foreseen) unpleasant side effects, especially if it is in the interests of employers to do so. Similarly, the voters may not be informed. Voters are informed by the media and if the media are ignorant or (worse) deliberately mislead them, voters will not be able to make a rational choice between alternative policies.

Recent legislation on freedom of information must surely be welcomed by Humanists but it is important to ensure that this initiative is fully implemented. Humanists think that strengthening democratic institutions is the most effective way of encouraging a sense of responsibility and this must be accompanied by free access to information: too often, even in democracies, governments try to conceal information from the public. It may be objected that one citizen has little influence on public affairs but in a democracy there are many ways in which public opinion can make itself felt. Letters can be written to politicians and to the press, pressure groups can be formed which, if successful, have their message taken up by the media (this is the modern substitute for holding public meetings, a procedure that television has made almost obsolete, except on a very small scale).

In conclusion it would seem that when things go wrong in society it is unreasonable to pin the blame on to any one person or group, such as scientists. In a democracy, a large number of people and groups are responsible for mistakes or the unforeseen consequences of their actions.

14 SCIENCE AND RELIGION
Are science and religion compatible?

HUMANISTS THINK THAT SCIENCE and theistic religions are not compatible because their approaches to basic beliefs are so different.

The religious approach is based on faith and most religious beliefs such as the existence of God, heaven, hell and the validity of divine revelation are untestable by scientific method. Humanists fully realise that over the last century or so, theological ideas have changed. For example, the Darwinian theory of evolution has now been accepted by most Christian sects and the Genesis story is now regarded as a myth except by creationists, especially in North America. This has led to the very real difficulty of knowing what theologians do believe. It is a common experience for Humanists to explain why they do not accept some particular theological belief only to be told that many theologians have long since given up that belief themselves! Even if theologians, following the example of scientists, have dropped or modified many old concepts, the ideas they still *do* accept are based either on religious experience – which however convincing to those who have them, are of no evidential value to others – or on faith, or on modern interpretation of the scriptures.

On the other hand, science relies on observed facts and experiments for support. Its hypotheses and conclusions are always based on probability, never on certainty. Old ideas are amended or replaced in the light of new knowledge.

A possible explanation for religious experience

The brains of a group of skilled meditators were scanned during meditation and the results showed intense activity in some parts of the brain and reduced activity in other parts. This was interpreted as the formation of a religious experience arising from the active part of the brain and the suppression of irrelevant thoughts in the quiescent part. Many people, including some Humanists, have reported having experienced an intense sensation, a sudden surge of pleasure, an overpowering feeling of wellbeing brought on by viewing a beautiful sunset, a thrilling musical performance, an impressive painting or other work of art, or some intense emotional incident. Sensations such as these may perhaps have been interpreted in former times by the devout as a religious experience.

This state of mind – what a well-known Humanist has suggested calling, with some reluctance, 'Humanist mysticism' – is by no means uncommon. But scientists (who may also enjoy these experiences) would more prosaically argue that they can be explained physiologically by the natural stimulation of the pleasure centre in the brain resulting in the release of neuro-transmitters, especially serotonin, sometimes called 'the feel-good chemical' which is associated with feelings of serenity and optimism.

Attempts to reconcile science and religion

In spite of the conflict between science and religion some scientists do adhere to Christianity or other theistic religions. How do they reconcile these two very different points of view? The following are among the most popular attempts to make this reconciliation although Humanists do not think any of them are valid.

Some scientists have two watertight compartments in their minds and make no attempt to fit together their religious and scientific views. Newton and Faraday were two such scientists. This is understandable because when they lived, the two main scientific ideas that conflict with the Bible, that is, the evolution of life and the great age of the Earth, had not been developed. It is more difficult to understand how a scientist can hold this position today, although some do: when asked about this, a common reply is along the lines that religious beliefs are 'too personal a matter to discuss'.

A more rational attempt to reconcile religious and scientific views is often referred to as 'the God of the gaps'. This means that although science can explain many things, a problem may eventually be reached which science cannot solve. Until very recently, science could offer no hypothesis to explain how matter/energy was created in the first place (*one has now been proposed, see page 22*). Certain steps in the evolution of complex living matter from non-living organic compounds cannot yet be explained (*see page 31*) and virtually nothing is known about how consciousness (the awareness of ourselves and our surroundings) is produced. Other gaps in our knowledge involve the origin of the scientific laws which were presumably fixed before matter was created. An allied problem is how the numerical values of fundamental constants, such as the speed of light, came into existence. If science cannot answer these questions then the intervention of God is suggested. However, as science progresses, more and more gaps are being filled. Some scientists have proposed there may be what is called a 'theory of everything' – a comprehensive, background theory from which the laws of physics, and perhaps the values of the constants, can be deduced. Efforts have been made to search for such a theory, although its existence is still speculative (and at least one scientist, Stephen Hawking, has abandoned the search).

A century ago, scientific knowledge was limited to the educated few. Widespread scientific thinking is a very youthful activity and future scientists may provide more answers. At the same time, we must accept human limitation: there is no reason to expect that the human intellect will ever by able to answer all fundamental questions.

Some scientists, although not necessarily accepting all the beliefs of a particular religion, think that the human mind needs a 'something' more ethereal and mystical than the matter-of-fact approach of science. They find religious practices to be emotionally satisfying, fulfilling some indefinable need. A psychologist once said that, as the human mind could not think rationally all the time, he went to church every Sunday to get his weekly dose of irrationality! Many

Humanists also often feel the need for what some would regard as non-rational or unwinding activities and meet this by taking part in such leisure occupations as fell walking (even in uncomfortable conditions!), taking pride in gardening, learning to play unusual musical instruments, researching the history of a locality, listening to jazz....

Another attempt to reconcile science and religion suggests they are about different things: science is about facts and religion is about values. While there is some truth in this, Humanists would point out that Christians claim that their religion is based on belief in the alleged historical facts of the birth, death and resurrection of Jesus Christ. Some of these beliefs are not only outside our experience but completely contrary to it: hence the scepticism of Humanists. Humanists think that they have a guide to moral values independently of divine revelation, namely, that we should consider how our actions affect the wellbeing of others. The suggested contrast between the content of religion (values) and science (facts) is not therefore clear-cut.

Other scientists explain modestly that a scientific training does not enable them to express opinions on religious matters any more than a theological training enables a person to express an opinion on science. So they assume that theologians 'know what they are talking about' and accept their views. Humanists would reply that scientists are entitled to express opinions on the factual statements that Christianity has traditionally accepted (and there is doubt as to how many Christians accept the truth of them today). The probability, for example, of the virgin birth, the resurrection and the after-life is becoming less and less as our knowledge grows. Scientists are also entitled to point out the difference between belief based on scientific method and belief based on faith.

It has been suggested that religious belief in the unseen is not qualitatively different from that of some of the beliefs of scientists. Theologians talk about the soul, divine revelation and eternal life etc. whilst the scientists talk about electrons, neutrons and black holes. It must be admitted that some ideas emanating from quantum theory are as much contrary to everyday experience as are many mystical religious beliefs! However, although the scientist deals with things that are unseen, they are based either on experimental evidence or on deductions from this evidence and ideas about them change in the light of new knowledge. Although some theological ideas have changed (usually from the impact of science) such things as belief in a personal God are still based ultimately on faith. Scientists suggest tentative hypotheses and if experiments do not decide which hypothesis is correct, they accept that the answer is not at present known.

A modern view about God as a designer which some scientists support is based on what is called *the anthropic principle*. This is a group of ideas defined in different ways by different authors (and described by one writer as a 'chaos of concepts'!). Many of the arguments are highly technical (for a popular account, see *Cosmic Coincidences* by John Gribbon and Martin Rees) but the one most readily understood points out that if the two opposing forces that operated during and after the Big Bang had not been so delicately balanced, the universe could not have developed in a way that permitted the formation of living things. The outward force of the Big Bang projecting the newly-formed matter in all directions as space expanded was opposed by the force of gravity that causes particles to attract each other and to cling together. If gravity had only been slightly more powerful (or the Big Bang slightly less powerful) then the particles would never have separated sufficiently to form the widely spaced galaxies that eventually produced stars, planets and – at least on our planet – living things. On the other hand, if gravity had been only slightly less powerful (or the Big Bang more powerful) matter would have been forced apart too rapidly to coalesce into galaxies and would remain as an ever-expanding cloud of gas. The fact that these forces were *just right* to allow both the dispersion of matter and its eventual collecting together as galaxies is taken as evidence of the existence of a designer, as the possibility that this balance could occur by chance is considered to be extremely remote. This is only one of several remarkable coincidences upon which the existence of life has depended.

One attempt to counter the idea that the anthropic principle involves a designer is the 'many universes' hypothesis. It is suggested that as millions of other island universes are known to exist (*see page 21*) then it is reasonable to speculate that many of these might have a different balance of forces – although we have no way of checking this. That the conditions on our planet happen to favour life could therefore be entirely due to nothing more than chance.

So, because Humanists think these arguments are unconvincing, they consider science and religion to be fundamentally incompatible. It is fully realised that Christian theologians now make more use of scientific method in exploring some aspects of the historical basis of Christianity, for example, archaeological studies of the Middle East and the rejection of the Genesis account of the world's origin. Humanists welcome the application of science to religious problems.

The value of religion

Humanists do not deny the value of religion to many people as a source of comfort, uplifting ideas and moral inspiration. Humanists, too, derive comfort and inspiration from their own views. Once they have adjusted to their conclusion that humankind cannot call on divine help but must work out its own destiny, Humanists receive great uplift by reflecting on human scientific achievement and responding to the moral challenge of trying to raise the general level of human wellbeing. In view of the value of religion to its adherents, the Humanist movement makes no attempt to convert religious people to Humanism. The Humanist message is directed to people who have lost their faith or who have never had one.

Attempts to test the effectiveness of prayer

Although Humanists do not accept the value of prayer as religious people understand it, there is one way in which it might be effective – as a placebo. A placebo is a preparation containing no active drugs which when given to patients who believe it *is* active often reduces their symptoms. Prayers for personal success, such as passing an examination or running a race, might have a similarly positive effect. It seems likely that when a congregation prays repeatedly for money for church or charitable purposes, then individuals feel motivated to contribute more to the funds.

The whole concept of prayer, and the necessity for it, is difficult to reconcile with the idea of the existence of a loving heavenly Father. There seems an inherent contradiction between an all-powerful all-seeing supreme being who needs to be asked for the basic necessities of life (even our daily bread!) and to be praised for supplying them. On the other hand, religious people might regard testing the efficacy of prayer as sacrilegious or even sinful (that is, contrary to the will of God).

There is statistical evidence that religious people, who are regular churchgoers who regularly pray, live longer than non-churchgoers, but there are several possible reasons for this. They enjoy and feel comfortable with church attendance and benefit from the friendship of like-minded people and their participation in charitable and similar activities. Also, absent members of the congregation might not go to church because of their ill-health, which may also be not unrelated to their earlier death. Religious faith also involves a placebo effect – (if you think God is looking after you, then you feel looked after!). Some reports from American medical schools suggest that religious belief has a beneficial effect on health. In one study, patients who believed in God were reported to have one third the mortality rate after heart by-pass surgery compared with those without religious belief: this could be a placebo effect.

In one study, begun in 1999, the medical progress of 1800 patients who had undergone heart surgery was compared. The patients were divided into three groups; two of these groups being prayed for by a team of intercessors. In order to detect a possible placebo effect, only one group was informed of the prayers. The third group was a control to indicate the normal rate of recovery without 'organised' prayers being said on their behalf (but of course there is no control of prayers by the patients themselves or their relatives). This study was well-designed and the numbers were impressive. But despite a statement that the experiment would finish by 2001, no results have so far been published.

In another study, on the death-rate of 232 elderly patients during the six months after cardiac open surgery, the result was found to be significantly related to whether the patients participated in social or community groups and what they described as 'the strength and comfort of religious belief.' The percentage of deaths were as follows: No group participation, and no religion, 20%. Social activity, no religion 8%. No social activity but religious comfort, 8%. Both group activity and religion, 3%. This clearly shows the interaction of group activity with religious belief, but leaves open the question of the effect on mortality of the religious belief itself.

Although the figures kept by closed religious communities such as Mormons and Seventh Day Adventists seem to indicate they live longer than the general population, the explanation could well be their lifestyle – no alcohol, no smoking or recreational drugs, simple and nutritious food, marriage at a young age, and much community support.

An attempt to investigate the efficacy of prayer was reported by Galton as long ago as 1883. It was pointed out that members of royal families were prayed for every week by millions of church-goers using official prayer books. The longevity of 97 royals averaged 64.0 years, slightly lower than the average of 67.5 for about 6000 'other classes of persons' thus suggesting that prayer had no beneficial effect.

The results of a survey of over fifty other attempts to determine whether prayer influences the recovery from illness, apparently carried out inexpertly by church members, was indecisive. In some cases there were no controls, the rate of recovery was not measured quantitatively and a possible placebo effect was ignored.

In conclusion, there is at present no satisfactory evidence for the efficacy of prayer on illness, but some observers have suggested that more carefully controlled tests on a larger scale would be justified.

Further reading
Gribbin, John and Rees, Martin   *Cosmic Coincidences*
(Black Swan, 1991)
Kurtz, Paul (ed)   *Science and Religion; are they compatible ?*
(Prometheus Books 2003)
See in particular Chapter 28: Tessman, Iwin and Tessman, Jack   *Efficacy of Prayer*
Lofmark, Carl   *Does God Exist?*
(Rationalist Press Association, 1999)
Lofmark, Carl   *What is the Bible?*
(Rationalist Press Association, 1999)
Warburton, Nigel   *Philosophy: The Basics*   (Chapter 2)
(Routledge, 1995)
Books by scientists who accept Christianity:
Polkinghorne, John   *Science and Christian Belief*
(SPCK, 1994)
Wilkinson, David and Frost, Rob   *Thinking Clearly about God and Science*
(Monarch Publications, 1996)

15 THE PROBLEM OF EVIL
What is the Humanist attitude to the problem of evil?

FOR THE HUMANIST, the *theological* problem of evil does not exist. This problem is how can the existence of undeserved pain, disease, disaster and misery be reconciled with a loving and all-powerful heavenly Father?

The existence of a good and all-powerful God is not logically compatible with a world in which there is widespread evil. If God is all-powerful and allows so much evil to exist He cannot be loving and if He is loving in the presence of evil he cannot be all-powerful. There have been many attempts to solve this problem, one of the most commonly quoted being that we should have faith in God whose ways are beyond human understanding. But theologians admit that there is no completely satisfactory answer.

The problem does not exist for Humanists because they see no evidence for a loving all-powerful God, or any god, to account for the existence of the universe and all the evil it contains.

The nature of evil

In Christian, Jewish and Muslim traditional beliefs, Satan was created a good angel who rebelled against God and his creatures, including humanity. He was cast out of heaven and became the promoter of evil, working through evil spirits whom the present Pope is reported to have said 'we call demons' and 'demons do exist'.

There does not seem to be any consensus among present-day Christians about the fundamental nature of evil. To Humanists, evil is simply natural phenomena such as earthquakes, floods, famines and the results of human wrong-doing, which reduce the well-being of humanity and of sentient animals. The problem for Humanists is: what actions should be taken to prevent, or alleviate the results of, those things that religious people regard as evil?

The many events and influences in the world that reduce the welfare and happiness of mankind do not therefore present a special philosophical problem to Humanists: they regard them simply as part of existence.

Modern science and technology can do a great deal to avoid natural disasters, or reduce their effects. Floods can be prevented by increasing drainage and maintaining forests, the effect of droughts can be prevented by building dams and by irrigation. Earthquakes and volcanic eruptions can, in some cases, now be predicted so that warnings can be issued and emergency services alerted, as is also possible with severe weather conditions such as hurricanes or blizzards. The movement of epidemics over continents is predictable so that medicines to prevent and cure them can be prepared in advance. Thus, the impact of many events that were major disasters in the past is now being reduced.

One of the greatest developments of the twentieth century has been the rapid rise in the study of social sciences which, it is hoped, will eventually bring within our grasp the control of many man-made problems such as war, poverty, crime, accidents and pollution. The signs are that humankind is beginning to learn that its prosperity, and possibly its survival, depends on more international co-operation. The existence of the United Nations provides a machinery, if still very imperfect, for dealing with international disputes. Modern knowledge of economics suggests that we have the means to achieve prosperity and avoid the extremes of rich and poor not only within nations but also between nations. Unfortunately the political will to apply this knowledge is still lacking.

Humanists, by freeing their minds from the theological approach to evil, are better able to concentrate their energy on how to deal with natural and man-made catastrophes.

The Christian and Humanist views on the nature of humankind

The Christian view of humankind is that it is a fallen species of miserable sinners who can achieve nothing on its own but must constantly seek God's help. To Humanists, this view is as psychologically damaging as it is lacking in evidence. Living things have, for millions of years, obtained their food and shelter, reproduced their kind and evolved into fitter species, but until the arrival of civilised humanity, neither one syllable of petitionary prayer nor a single paean of praise was offered to God. Why therefore is it thought that humankind, the most able of all species, cannot survive or develop without God's help? Although fully realising that some people behave in an antisocial manner and that much suffering arises from human action, Humanists regard the human race as a magnificent species, capable of immense feats of creativity, invention, organisation and benevolence – and unique in that it can exert some control over its evolution and destiny. Civilised humanity has existed for less than about 10,000 years and is still in its infancy compared with many other species, some of which have existed for millions of years. Serious study and action to alleviate disease, misery and poverty on an international scale are very recent developments, some measured only in decades. In spite of severe human and natural disasters during the 1990s there has been a steady improvement in the human lot in many parts of the world during the twentieth century. Humanists do not claim the power of prophecy, but the increased concern for human suffering gives ground for hope that along with modern scientific developments many of the challenges which now face humanity will be effectively met in the thousands of years that probably lie ahead of the human race.

16 FREE WILL AND DETERMINISM
What is the Humanist attitude to free will and determinism?

FREE WILL IS THE BELIEF that people have liberty to choose the way they behave. Determinism, on the other hand, implies that people have no freedom of choice and that their actions are determined by the influence of their genes and of their environment, over which they have no control.

In Europe, this debate came into prominence with the introduction of Christianity. The Christians thought in terms of an all-powerful God that controlled the universe and everything in it. This meant that humankind was controlled by God and therefore had no personal choice about its own thoughts and behaviour. St Augustine (354 – 430) was the first Christian writer to realise that this led to an impossible paradox. He thought that humanity had free will, but also believed in an all-powerful God. He failed to solve the problem: if humankind is free, how can God be all-powerful?

The issue of free will versus determinism does not arise until we consider the state of organisation of matter/energy in the human body and perhaps the higher animals. In the realm of non-living matter and of most living things, determinism is generally assumed to operate. (In the interests of strict accuracy, it should be mentioned that quantum theory postulates that the behaviour of electrons is not determined, but this is not relevant in any practical way to objects in everyday life). Human beings, with their development of thought and imagination, *think* that they have the ability to choose between several courses of action. But is this impression that we are free to choose what we do, an illusion? It is obvious that some circumstances of our lives are determined by our heredity and environment. For example, anyone born in a remote Third World village will have a very different behaviour pattern and outlook on life compared with someone born in a prosperous European town. The question is whether *all* our decisions and conduct are completely determined by our genes and past experience.

The argument between free will and determinism still goes on after many centuries and the thinking on both sides is subtle. It is a philosophical and not a scientific question in that it depends on argument and speculation and cannot be tested by any obvious experiments. There is no space here to analyse the problem and to summarise the lengthy and complicated arguments but it can be said that neither side has won and this problem may never be solved. Although some Humanists may favour the determinist position philosophically, in everyday life they assume that people have free will and legally they are expected to bear the full responsibility for what they do and how they behave. The courts now accept 'diminished responsibility' or 'extenuating circumstances' as a defence (that is, they accept that the behaviour of some people may be determined by genetic and environmental influences and that they lack the free will that the majority are assumed to have).

A further irony is that if determinists are correct, they do not arrive at their decisions after carefully weighing up the arguments. On their own admission, they are compelled to reach that conclusion by their genetic make-up and their previous experiences! If determinists are right, we are mere puppets and any discussion of moral principles is simply a charade controlled by our determined lines of thought. Whilst this possibility cannot be denied, and we have no rational means of deciding the issue, Humanists accept in practice our clear impression that we have an element of free will and can exert some decisive influence over our own actions.

Some religious teaching has taken the line that everything that happens has been in the mind of God since the beginning of time and that it cannot be changed. This can lead to the idea that there is no point in making any effort to change our living conditions because the future is fixed. The effect of this is to induce people to be fatalistic and to submit to poverty, squalor and disease instead of working to improve conditions so as to raise the quality of human life. Humanists emphatically reject this line of thinking.

17 THE MEANING AND PURPOSE OF LIFE
What do Humanists think are the meaning and purpose of life? Why does the world exist?

HUMANISTS REALISE THAT THEY cannot discern any meaning or purpose in the universe, the existence of which they regard as an inexplicable mystery and they are prepared to live with this. In the pre-scientific age it was taken for granted that the universe was created by God for the benefit of humanity but science has shown that, on the scale of the universe as a whole, humankind is utterly insignificant in both space and time. People who believe in a divine creator may think that the creator had some purpose in mind but that purpose is far from clear. The short answer is, therefore, that Humanists are not able to see any long-term meaning or purpose in the universe, and are content to accept this.

Scientists predict that there will come a time, thousands of millions of years hence, when all life on earth will cease as the sun expands into a red giant star and overheats, or even engulfs, the earth. On the astronomical time scale, it could be argued that life has no purpose because of its eventual extinction. However, we are not concerned with such a time scale in everyday life and if we consider the present and immediate future of individuals it is assumed that they seem to be able, to a large extent, to choose their own purpose in life. Some may consider their careers as their main activity, others may give priority to raising a family while yet others may give their main energies into hobbies and sports. In other words, life can have a very real purpose, or combine several purposes in each individual.

Humankind is still a youthful species

Although the human species separated from its ape-like ancestors about two millions of years ago, humankind has known civilisation for less than 10,000 years and what might be called modern technological humanity is a very youthful type indeed, being scarcely a century old. Humanity may reasonably expect to survive for many thousands of years, although during this time there may be need to cope with some serious set-backs. Assuming collisions with extra-terrestrial bodies, and natural disasters (*such as those mentioned on page 25*) do not occur, the increasing likelihood of global warming and the long-term effects of environmental pollution on human health, to say nothing of pandemics and the spread of Aids are all threats which cannot be ignored. But the total effect of improvements in the human environment from discoveries, inventions and the more equitable political and social structures introduced now or in the near future could be enormous when measured in terms of the permanent benefit to countless future generations. Surely this thought provides a most challenging incentive for action and a most worthwhile purpose in life!

Why does Earth exist?

This is a reasonable question to ask by anyone who believes in a God who created the universe, as presumably He must have had some purpose in mind when He created Earth. The traditional view, dating from the time when it was believed that our planet was the centre of the universe, has been that God created it to provide a home for humankind. But this leaves unanswered the question: Why did He do this? As Humanists reject the idea of a Creator and it is now known our planet is an insignificant speck in an unimaginably vast universe, this idea about the purpose of Earth is unacceptable. The only frank answer that the Humanist can give is that there is no information on which to base a conjecture as to why Earth, or indeed the cosmos, exists.

18 DEATH (AND LIFE AFTER DEATH?)
Do Humanists believe in life after death?

THE SHORT ANSWER IS 'NO'. And it may be added neither do they believe in life before birth – the idea that individual personalities have lived before (reincarnation). However, this short answer needs some amplification.

To maintain life, the organism must take in food and oxygen for body building and the provision of energy. This internal chemical activity is called *metabolism* and while the organism is alive its metabolism maintains a balance between the intake of food, water and oxygen for growth and the output of energy and waste. In human beings, when the oxygen supply to the brain stops for more than a few minutes the brain cells begin to deteriorate and soon cease to control the body. When the control finally ends it is impossible to restart it and the body is dead. After death, the body soon begins to decompose into simpler compounds which eventually become available to plants and other animals thus completing the cycle of life. What remains? Humanists find it difficult to believe that anything remains other than the memories of the individual and the effects and influences of their achievements. As has been stated elsewhere there is no scientific evidence for the existence of a soul and it is difficult to believe that the mind can exist independently of the body.

However, in two respects people can live on after their death. In the first place, sexual reproduction means that some of the characteristics of parents are passed on through their genes to their offspring and to future generations. Secondly, with the development of speech, writing, drawing and other modern methods of recording, many people have had and will continue to have great influence after their deaths. Dawkins has coined the word *memes* (from *memory* and *genes*) to indicate that new ideas by spreading from brain to brain can replicate (like genes) and have an ever-widening influence through present and future generations.

Two important conclusions result from the Humanist attitude to death. Humanists do not expect a future life of bliss in a heaven or torment in hell. Humanists concentrate on aiming to improve the quality of life on earth – as it is the only life we are sure about.

Reincarnation

In recent years there has been a renewed interest in reincarnation – the idea that after a person's death their soul returns to life in a new-born baby. There are reports of people, sometimes under hypnosis, claiming to have recollections of events in a former existence – although it is possible that these people have read or heard about these events and forgotten them and later recalled them from their memory. Humanists do not consider this evidence – the examples are too few and uncertain – to be a serious challenge to their disbelief in the after-life. A further difficulty with belief in reincarnation is that, as the population of the world is increasing, the number of babies being born is larger than the number of people dying.

Humanist funeral ceremonies

As Humanists do not believe that humankind survives after death, it naturally follows that Humanists do not think that prayers and funeral ceremonies have any effect on the dead. Funerals are for the benefit of the living and can have a role in relieving tension, coming to terms with grief and providing an opportunity for paying a tribute to the deceased and offering consolation to relatives and friends.

Many people realise that the conventional religious funeral is completely inappropriate for anyone who does not believe in the after-life or regularly attend a place of worship. The alternative for a bereaved Humanist family is a non-religious funeral ceremony (perhaps it should not be called a service). Such a ceremony can typically include a summary of the deceased's life and achievements, perhaps with special reference to their contribution to Humanist ideals. In addition, there would be words of comfort (sometimes consisting of poems or quotations from well-known sources) to friends and relatives. A list of people willing to conduct secular funerals, as well as marriages and naming ceremonies, is available from the British Humanist Association (address in appendix). Requests are welcomed but it is not always possible to provide these ceremonies in all parts of the country. The BHA has also published a useful booklet, *Funerals without God*, which includes suggested formats for secular funerals along with poems and quotations suitable for inclusion.

The biological significance of death

Death has important biological and sociological consequences. If people continued to be born and never died the world would rapidly become over-populated. Also, evolution depends on the death and replacement of successive generations.

Parapsychology and the question of survival

Parapsychology (now known as *psi*) is the study of various inexplicable phenomena, real or supposed, some of which are relevant to the question of survival after death.

Over the centuries, many people have reported going through an experience described as 'seeing a ghost' especially in some building or location reputed to be 'haunted'. Although the occurrence of these experiences cannot be denied, their cause or causes are highly controversial. In many cases, they may arise from optical illusions, hallucinations or other natural events. When under emotional stress, some people have difficulty in separating reality from fantasy. Scientific studies have not led to any conclusion about the reality and nature of these experiences but they provide no evidence for the popular explanation that 'ghosts' are the spirits of dead people.

Spiritualism is a religious movement whose adherents believe in the afterlife and that specially sensitive people (*mediums*) can communicate with the dead. Some of these claims (but not all) have been exposed as frauds and many communications are so vague as to have no evidential value. Again, scientific investigations have failed to establish either the validity of the messages or their source. One approach to the question of survival attempted by a few scientists has been to leave a sealed or coded message with the object of challenging mediums to see whether they can receive the message or crack the code after the experimenter had died. There are no reports of a successful outcome.

Laboratory studies in psi

In recent years many rigorously controlled scientific studies have been carried out on psi. The two main topics have been extra sensory perception (ESP) – the alleged ability to obtain information from sources other than the normal senses – and telekinesis – the alleged ability of mind to affect matter, for example, by determining whether it is possible to influence by thought the output of machines generating random numbers. Small but statistically significant results have been reported and are unexplained. The results of psi experiments have been inconclusive, partly because of the failure of different groups of workers to replicate each other's results: also, a common finding is that workers who believe in the validity of psi obtain positive results while the results of sceptics are negative (the sheep and goat effect).

If these organised laboratory experiments cannot produce agreed results it is not surprising that the study of spontaneous phenomena – poltergeists, ghosts, and messages from spiritualist mediums – have been equally inconclusive.

Death-bed experiences

The reported experiences of dying people, and especially those who, with modern medical technology, have been resuscitated after short periods of apparent death, have shown remarkable similarities. One group of reports mentions an 'out of body experience' (OBE) in which the individuals appear to have floated above their bodies and were able to see and hear doctors and nurses trying to revive them and, in some cases, pronouncing them to be dead. Other experiences are of passing along a dark passage with lights at the end, of seeing relatives who were already dead and of a feeling of intense peace and serenity (so much so that a few patients were quite resentful that they had been resuscitated!). Although these experiences have been quoted as evidence for the entry of the dying into another world it is well-established that one effect of lack of oxygen (which occurs with failing circulation as death approaches) is hallucination and a feeling of elation. Lack of oxygen might therefore explain these experiences.

Scientific attitudes to psi

Many people dismiss the subject of psi as 'impossible' because it seems to contradict their whole pattern of thought. On the other hand, some people – including some scientists – welcome the study of this subject: they argue that if *any* of the claims of psi prove to be true they would have a great influence on scientific and philosophical thought.

Further reading
James Alcock, Jean Burns, Anthony Freeman (eds) *Psi Wars*
(Imprint Academic, 2003)
Ellison, Arthur J *Science and the Paranormal : Altered States of Reality*
(Floris Books, 2002)
Moody, Raymond A *Reflections on Life After Life*
(Mockingbird Books 1977)
Rhine, J B *New Frontiers of the Mind*
(Penguin 1950)
and *The Reach of The Mind*
(Penguin 1954)
Stevenson, Ian *Twenty Cases Suggestive of Reincarnation*
(Virginia University Press, 1974)
Stevenson, Ian *European Cases of the Reincarnation Type*
(McFarland and Company, 2003)

Wambach, Helen *Life Before Life*
(Bantam Books, 1979)
Wynne Wilson, Jane *Funerals Without God: a practical guide to non-religious funeral ceremonies*
(BHA 1995)
Wynne Wilson, Jane *Sharing the Future: a practical guide to non-religious wedding ceremonies*
(BHA 1996)
Wynne Wilson, Jane *New Arrivals: non-religious baby namings*
(BHA 1999)

19 WORLD POPULATION TRENDS

How can human welfare be improved in view of the world's growing population and the reduced birth rates in some countries?

THE WORLD'S POPULATION almost doubled in the nineteenth century (it rose from 840 billion to 1550 billion) and quadrupled during the twentieth century from 1550 to 6000 billion, mostly in developing countries). The population is still rising, although the *rate* of growth is falling, and the United Nations estimate that it will be 2050 before it reaches its peak (of 9.3 billion) and the size of the world population begins to fall. Another estimate suggests the peak will not be reached until 2070.

Following the 'green revolution' – the dramatic increase in productivity in some developing countries from the introduction of high-yielding grain varieties and the use of fertilisers, pesticides and improved irrigation – it has been possible in recent decades to increase food production sufficiently to provide for most of the present population, at least at the subsistence level. While famines have occurred, these have been caused by wars, floods or droughts rather than by population pressure. Owing to the limited infrastructure in African agriculture, that continent derived little benefit from the green revolution.

The reasons for the rise in population during the nineteenth century is that in developing countries, as European countries were at that time, a large family could be an economic asset. It costs little to educate and provided a free labour force for producing the family's food, or helping with a family business or working in the expanding industries. It also provided a miniature built-in welfare state as some members of the family could act as child minders and others care for the elderly. In highly developed countries, however, bringing up and educating children is very expensive and few parents can expect their children to contribute regularly to the family income or look after them in old age. These considerations, along with the availability of contraception, led to the reduction of family size in the twentieth century.

In spite of the improved nutrition resulting from the green revolution, there are still some parts of the world in which food supplies are inadequate. Many estimates suggest maldistribution is the problem, rather than lack of production. Developed countries produce more food than they need, but using this surplus to make up the shortfall in developing countries is not practicable. Apart from the difficulty and expense of transporting their surplus, western foods are not always acceptable elsewhere; for example, the many millions whose basic food is either rice or maize are unprepared to substitute wheat. In a world of overall plenty, it has been estimated (August 2004) that about 400 million people are malnourished. The provision of adequate food, along with the reduction of poverty, presents the world with two of its greatest challenges.

A meeting in Narobi in September 2004 aimed to co-ordinate the activities of UN agencies (WHO, FAO and UNESCO) and the World Bank. It expected to learn from the experience of Vietnam, Thailand and China, countries which have succeeded in increasing agricultural output. This endeavour may help to reduce malnutrition and raise the income of impoverished farmers by means of increasing food supplies, increasing soil fertility and limiting erosion, combating pests and diseases and reducing losses of stored food. The world research budget for agriculture is estimated to be 33b$ per year, the estimated costs of setting up the global partnership (55m$) should be easily affordable. It is to be hoped that these initiatives will be more successful than previous endeavours of this kind.

Meanwhile the increase in population will continue. It is expected that another billion will be living in Africa by 2050. In India the population is expected to overtake that of China to become the world's most populous country.

Falling birth-rates

In strong contrast to the rising populations of many developing countries, elsewhere the birth-rate is falling.

The stability of any population depends on the average number of children produced by a woman in her lifetime (the replacement fertility rate, *rfr*). The figure for a stable population is not exactly 2.0 as might be expected, as allowance must be made for members of the population who decide not to have children, or who die childless. Assuming a stable death rate, the population will rise if the rfr is higher than 2.1; if below, it will fall. By 1995, the rfr was below 2.1 in 59 countries (such as: Italy 1.2, Germany 1.29, Canada 1.58, Britain 1.6, USA 1.93). Even in countries with large populations, the rfr fell between 1980 and 2000 as follows: Pakistan from 7.0 to 5.5, India 4.7 to 3.0, Vietnam 5.7 to 2.3 and Nigeria from 7.0 to 5.0. In some African countries, the population is falling from the high death-rate from Aids especially among the child-bearing population.

Reasons for the falling birth-rates

One important factor – apart from the increasing availability of contraceptives – is the improvements in the education and employment of women so that they have interests other than that of bringing up children. Many women rebel against the tedium and hard work involved in excessive child-bearing. Even in countries such as Italy, Iran and Brazil where contraception is strongly discouraged by religious influences, the fertility rate has also fallen which emphasises the importance of family choice (and the probable increasing influence of women in making that choice). As we have seen, urbanisation is another factor: a large family can be an economic asset on a farm but not so readily in an industrial town.

Consequences of the falling birth-rates

Within a few decades, the low birth-rates will have serious economic, political and social effects in many countries including

Britain. These will arise from an ageing population implying a loss of productivity, of initiative and new ideas. In 2001, for the first time, the over-60s out-numbered the under-16s and by 2014 more than one third of the population will be over 60. In 1951, there were 270 centenarians in Britain. This increased to 6000 in 2004 and, if this trend continues, will be 45,000 by 2030! At present, there are 3.35 people of working age for each pensioner, by 2011 this will change to 3.1 and by 2031 will be reduced to about 2.5. The pension industry in 2004 is already in trouble as pensioners live longer and take more from the funds with fewer young people paying into them. Future 30-to-55 age groups will not only have to meet the expenses of their children but may also be responsible for elderly parents.

Some possible solutions

The present tendency for early retirement could be reversed (people with jobs they like may welcome this but those with boring routine work would probably oppose it). An encouragement of immigration of young people from over-populated countries would be helpful but this might be only a short-term solution as it seems likely that the availability of such immigrants will diminish as the population in their own countries will eventually become unbalanced. The most basic solution would be policies aiming at increasing the fertility rate towards the vital 2.1, such as increases in family allowances and reduction in the costs of education. An increase in part-time work and flexible hours would also be expected to reverse the tendency for small families.

International efforts have been made to press governments of countries with a high birth-rate to encourage family planning. There are difficulties arising from religious doctrines, from unwillingness to change old customs or modes of thought; and many people resent being told what to do on such a personal matter as family size. Nevertheless, some countries have enforced family limitation and have met these difficulties.

Although some governments have taken steps to propose targets for reduced family size, it is of interest that the present widespread fall in birth-rates appears to have occurred from voluntary parental choice – a change which Humanists must welcome.

20 CONCLUSION

Humanism may be acceptable and satisfying to the learned scientist, but does it meet everybody's needs?

IT IS TRUE THAT HUMANIST ideas were originated by highly educated people as they were the first to see the difficulties of religious belief and were sufficiently independent to express their views without fear of the consequences. However, today many people with only a rudimentary knowledge of science find that religious beliefs strain their credulity. The decline of attendance at places of worship, particularly churches in most parts of the western world, suggests that many people can and do live their daily lives without any religious practices. On the other hand, some people who find it difficult to accept religious belief nevertheless feel that without it they have no anchor in life nor any basis for morals. Individuals who have been brought up with a religious faith which has gradually faded may need some mental readjustment to face up to the Humanist belief that the human race is alone and that there is no supernatural force that can be turned to for help.

The Humanist position is really very simple and can be understood by anyone. It emphasises that the here and now of this life is all that we can be sure of and that we should make the most of it. Humanist moral values, beginning with the surely indisputable belief that human well-being is to be preferred to human misery, provide a simple basis for a well-balanced life. Actions that raise the level of human wellbeing are right and good; those with the reverse effect are to be avoided and discouraged. The practical application of this can lead to many activities ranging from being friendly and helpful to a lonely neighbour to supporting and working for the various organisations concerned with raising living and health standards throughout the world.

Thus Humanism can give a sense of purpose and provide a background for a satisfying and exhilarating life for everybody.

Useful addresses

British Humanist Association,
1 Gower Street, London WC1E 6HD,
telephone 0207-793 3580

Gay and Lesbian Humanist Association
34 Spring Lane, Kenilworth,Warwickshire CVS 2HB,
telephone 01926-858 450

International Humanist and Ethical Union,
I Gower Street, London WC1E 6HD,
telephone 0207-631 3170

National Secular Society
25 Red Lion Square, London WC1R 4RL,
telephone 0207-404 3126

Rational Press Association
47 Theobalds Road, London WC1X 8SP,
telephone 0207-430 1371

Voluntary Euthanasia Society
13 Prince of Wales Terrace, London W8 5PG,
telephone 0207-937 7770

North East Humanists
Contact our website
hppt://NorthEast.Humanists.net
for up-to-date information.